RAISED BY
STRANGERS

one woman's spiritual journey home

Brooke Lynn

Torchflame Books
An imprint of Light Messages

Contents

Dedications

My Dear Husband, your love and loyalty has proven to be the strength I needed to keep on living. You have shown me grace, forgiveness and acceptance like no one else. You have helped me become the woman I am. God handpicked you to take on the challenging task of marrying me, and you do it with excellence. I've watched God greatly grow you and bless our marriage. You have added hope and value into my spirit which makes an eternal difference. Thank you for creating a Christian home and family with me. I am certain one day God will look into your eyes and say, "Well done my good and faithful servant." I love you!

My Children, you two are the greatest blessings in my life. I prayed for you and God gave me the desires of my heart. I'm proud to be your mom. Proud to have the opportunity to watch you grow up and become all God has made you to be. It's my aspiration to leave behind a Legacy of Love. You two are that legacy. Keep the flames burning. I can't wait to experience on this earth, and in eternity, the fruit of mine and your labor. Be bold, be strong and stay close to Jesus. I love you!

Heavenly Father, without You, I wouldn't have life, or a story to share of your love, hope, redemption and restoration. Forgive me for all the years I grieved my life and who I was. Thank you for making me who I am. I am wholly surrendered to you. I am grateful and honored to be your daughter. "For to me, to live is Christ and to die is gain." (Philippians 1:21 NIV)

Acknowledgements

Kelly Battles, you are my mentor, my friend, and an amazing editor. Thank you for believing in me. You are my number one cheerleader! This book was dormant until I met you; my words were sitting still and breathless. You helped make my dreams come true, bringing my words to life. You gave me hope and confidence, encouraging me that my book was worth writing, and something to share with the world. You radiate love, and your generosity and faithfulness make you a true woman after God's own heart. Thank you. I love you.

I would like to express my gratitude to Light Messages Publishing. You have been a guiding light, full of wisdom and resourceful information. You are an answer to prayer. You have made it possible for my story to reach thousands of people and I am extremely thankful for your help and generosity. Many lives will be changed because of your faithfulness. Thank you for turning my dreams into reality and publishing my book!

Preface

Our secrets remain locked away and tucked inside our souls. We keep the doors to our hearts bolted shut. We refuse to expose our pain, abuse, addictions, despair, and our past that makes us vulnerable. Because we fear disappointment, we don't find the strength to trust. We erect walls and refuse to restore relationships or build new ones to keep our hearts protected. We live in fear and pain from past failures, keeping us from taking a step forward in faith. I know this because of my own experiences. I was shut down, pushed down, and beaten up, abandoned, and shoved down a long road of pain and dysfunction. I am tired of hiding my pain. Finished with people looking at me and believing I have the perfect life, or I have it all together. There are no secrets here.

At five years old, I was kidnapped, abandoned, given away, and then raised by strangers. My childhood was saturated with physical and emotional pain as I endured dysfunction and mistreatment. It was only by grace, the invisible hands of God, and hope that I stayed alive. At the age of thirteen, what appeared as the light at the end of the tunnel only proved to be another pit of pain. My father had spent years searching for me with help from the police and the FBI. For him, it ended in a moment of relief and triumph. I was passed from the strangers in my life into his hands. However, this wasn't the "happily ever after" that I expected.

My desire for you as you read this book is that your impossible meets God and healing begins. I'm so excited for us to take this journey together. I've been waiting for you. My prayer is that you will come to the realization as I have that "hope is real and should never be denied."

~Brooke Lynn

Introduction

You are beautiful. You are loved. God made you perfect just the way you are. You are good enough. You are worth it, and your value is not estimated by your outward appearance. Whoever made you believe less or feel inadequate; shame on them. But it's time to move forward knowing and believing the truth about yourself. It's time to stand strong, believe in yourself, get healthy and be healthy because you love your life. No more living for societal approval. Hold your head up and know what God's word says about you. "You made all the delicate, inner parts of my body and knit me together in my mother's womb. Thank you for making me so wonderfully complex! Your workmanship is marvelous--how well I know it." (Psalm 139:13-14)

1

Almost Aborted

Woven in Love - Nurtured in Rebellion

*T*he enemy has tried so hard to steal, destroy, and kill me. He tried even before I was born by tempting my mother with the thoughts of having an abortion. She struggled internally and fought hard against every idea and plan to abort her pregnancy. She wondered if she could bring herself to take a life, or even physically endure the procedure. Her biggest apprehension was the inability to forgive herself. She feared she could never be forgiven.

Her Catholic upbringing pounded rules into her mind and heart. She sat desolate in her room and cried with her rosary in hand as tears streamed down her face and dripped off her cheeks, soaking the hardwood floor. Her mind raced with questions. "How could this happen to me? What have I done, and how will I survive such a fate?" She knew this was in fact her fault after giving into her own desires and the temptation to be with a man she believed she loved. Did her feelings betray her? How could a loving and caring God punish her with a pregnancy at the young age of seventeen? She peered down at her stomach while nausea overcame her, and she tried to envision a bump declaring to the world what had become of her. Thoughts whirled in her mind, her heart wavered, and only time would tell what decision she would make.

Her boyfriend charmed her with convincing words she wanted to hear. He pledged to provide for her and support her no matter what,

1

although his actions and demeanor proved otherwise. Abortion was on the table, and he agreed to help her commit this act. They could carry it out easily. He promised my mother the secret would remain theirs. No one would ever know. Or would they? She was scared, alone, and unable to trust anyone.

Early in the morning before the sun peeked over the horizon, my father quietly drove up her street and parked a couple houses down, just as planned. Mom dressed in jeans, a comfortable t-shirt, an oversized sweatshirt, ready for whatever the day would hold. She packed a few items in a small bag consisting of her needs for the clinic: her identification, cash, clean clothes, and feminine products. She included her mascara in case it ran down her face, and eye drops for red eyes. She was running late, but not because of any mishap. She was running late because every step she took and every move she made was like a slow motion movie playing in her head. Her mind was toying with her and creating an intense anxiety causing dizziness and her hands to tremble. She used the bathroom, checked the clock, grabbed her belongings, and headed for the front door. It took more effort than normal to reach the door; the hallway was longer and the darkness in the house was thick and eerie. When she reached for the front doorknob and tried to turn it, her hands trembled as she fell to her knees. Weakness took over her, and tears streamed like floodgates breaking forth. When she was able, she pulled herself together and went back to her room. She shut the bedroom door behind her, locked it, and lay on her bed face down into her pillows, sobbing.

The battle continued in my young mother's mind, and ultimately her conscience won out. She reached within herself and grabbed onto her dignity and her religion. She knew she couldn't live with herself for the rest of her life if she aborted her baby. At long last, she made the decision to keep the baby and be responsible.

God was pleased with her and her wise choice. With His hand upon her and her precious baby, God kept her joyful and strong through her circumstances and pain.

Unfortunately, Karl began cheating on her while they were dating. Her wild suspicions became reality when she began to notice hickies on his neck. Devastated, she confronted him, but he denied all her accusations and called my mom crazy to assume he would cheat. Even though he couldn't hide the undeniable truth and lie his way out, she chose to hide her pain and stay with him because of her desperate need for love and a father for her baby.

Karl harbored an explosive temper rearing its ugly head during their courting. One evening, a heated discussion became violent when he punched a mirror and needed medical attention in an emergency room. His injury resulted in surgery and sutures to fix his hand.

Karl portrayed himself as a man of honor and importance but he possessed an attitude of arrogance and lips that lied. He was emotionally manipulative. He made himself look good and responsible, but only to uphold a false sense of identity to others. Behind closed doors, he wasn't good. He was a troubled teenager who dropped out of high school in the spring of his graduating year. This greatly displeased his parents who gave him an ultimatum: join the military or become homeless. He chose to join the Navy, and since he was a minor at age seventeen, his parents signed the papers for him to enlist.

This man who would become my father was never prepared in mind or heart. Karl didn't come from a close-knit family. He had not known any love of his own; therefore, he had none to give. In the years to come, his brokenness and sorrow would break forth and lead him into a life of despair, ugliness, and loneliness. His actions wouldn't only affect himself, but also the people closest to him.

Woven in Love - Nurtured in Rebellion

Both just seventeen years old, my mother and father wed, but not just for the sake of love. They did so as a desperate measure to hide my existence. As minors in the state of New York, both of them had their mothers sign for them to marry. The secret remains until this day if either or both of my grandmothers knew of my mom's pregnancy.

Their marriage was also a deliberate act of disobedience against the will of my mom's dad. My grandfather greatly disliked my father because of his disrespectful attitude and his troubled behavior. Not only was my father a "drop out" from high school but he planned to run away with my mother. When my grandfather caught details of this plan, it infuriated him. He kept my mom home from school and called Karl's parents. My grandfather warned my mother Karl wasn't right for her.

My mother refused to heed his advice. The threat of being disowned by her own father was carried through because she defiantly surrendered herself to a man who promised to love, cherish, protect, and stand by her until death, a man who only offered empty and broken promises.

As for me, I was safe and secure in my mother's womb. I had a future and hope set before me. I was born on a warm and sunny spring day, in the state of Florida at the Pensacola Naval Hospital. I entered the world at 0508 weighing in at 7 pounds and 12 ounces. My mom endured fourteen hours of exhausting labor and was almost forced to have a c-section due to my position as a footling breach baby. She fearfully refused the c-section and miraculously delivered me as a difficult, but safe birth.

I was born into this world a sinner with an adequate amount of innocence, gently guided into the world by the hands of a physician and the God who created me. The doctor placed me into the tender hands of the one who carried me in her warm, secure womb. My mom was first to hold my precious life as she smiled and embraced me happily in her arms.

My life was almost taken away before it began. But make no mistake, God always has a plan. I'm thankful he holds me in the palm of His hand. My name is Brooke, and I have a purpose! "For I know the plans I have for you," says the LORD. "They are plans for good and not for disaster, to give you a future and a hope." (Jeremiah 29:11)

Linked by DNA

Karl was blonde, tall, and slender in appearance, and known for his pompous personality. My father was active duty in the Navy and worked in law enforcement. He looked good in his military uniform, as most men do. Women were attracted to him because he held a job in law enforcement, the confidence he carried in himself, and his deceitful ability to lure them in with whatever they needed to hear or whatever they wanted. Within the first two years of his marriage, he was accused and found guilty of having affairs with several women. While my father served a tour overseas, my mother received news by letter of her husband's appalling affairs. Karl's captain wrote home to make my mom aware her husband was cheating and to warn her, he had contracted an STD. Karl showed no dedication to his initial wife or family in which he had first made a covenant.

When Karl returned from overseas, my mother forgave him for what he had done, and they mended their differences. My mom became pregnant soon after his return. When I was two years old, I became a big sister. My mom gave birth to a son, my brother James.

Daddy Issues

My father made it clear to my mother she had to be dressed with make-up on before eight o'clock in the mornings. She was to keep the house clean always, and he dictated what to cook for dinner. Karl did the shopping on base and even bought Mom the make-up he wanted her to wear. He controlled the finances, and he wouldn't allow her to work. He was verbally abusive, calling my mom "fat" and demanded she lose weight. When my brother was only two months old, my father cheated on my mother again. This time it was with their next door neighbor.

Karl had a responsibility to take care of his wife and children, but instead he gave into the temptations of this world and his selfish desires. Wrecking havoc on his family, he found himself in court signing divorce papers, due to the emotional trauma he caused his wife. The judge granted the divorce in favor of my mother and praised her for her choice to leave such a man. Karl was ordered to pay child support and allowed visitation to us children on the weekends. When he picked us up on weekends, we either stayed with our grandparents without him, or he took us to his new girlfriend's apartment to play with her kids.

One Day Your Prince Will Come

Wounded, battered, and torn apart, six months after her divorce was final, my mother found love, acceptance, and affirmation in another man. My mom's new boyfriend Marc was a spark of hope in her eyes. He charmed her with his tough and strong personality. She felt secure and protected in his presence, but in reality she was weak and broken in her state of mind. Marc promised her a life of happiness and to help take care of her and her children. My mom completely surrendered herself into the arms of her new lover. She took refuge in him and believed in him with all her heart.

Marc was from New Mexico. He'd been traveling for work with a construction company when my mom met him at an amusement park. He didn't have a home of his own and had been living with his parents in New Mexico. Marc and my mom dated in New York about four months before he proposed we all move to New Mexico with him. He invited us to live with his family until he settled into a place of his own.

Amber Alert

When I was five years old my mother did the unthinkable and kidnapped me and my brother. She left my father and the state of New York and ran away with us and her new lover. With abounding hope and extravagant promises of a better life than she had previously, all four of us ventured onto a Greyhound bus bound for New Mexico. My mom, her lover, my brother, and I began an adventure to start our lives over, taking nothing with us except the rights of my father who knew nothing about our departure. We ventured off into the night vanishing from his reach and sight. Never again would my father be the same after the betrayal of his ex-wife. When she stole his children, this left him with bitterness, anger, and unforgiveness he carries until this day. He was left in a situation without any control, and he blamed my mother for everything.

Hell-O New Mexico

As I stepped off the bus into the New Mexico heat, I felt an odd tightness in my chest and found it difficult to breathe. Maybe it was anxiety, or possibly the heat from the desert air. Regardless of the cause, it was ironically symbolic of the hell I was about to begin living. My mother had no plans for how she would care for us children. She was without a job and had no friends or family to help her. The only person she had to support her was her boyfriend, Marc, who in turn had nothing himself except his parents and a sister.

The four of us sat down in the Greyhound station restaurant. We all sat together at a table, appearing as a "normal" family. Funny thing is we were the furthest thing from a real family. On the table there was no food, just drinks. I don't remember the last time I had eaten on the trip. Maybe it was some snacks on the bus-ride. The ice-cold pop was refreshing and cooled me down. My brother and I ran around the restaurant, chasing each other and laughing. We made frequent visits to the pop machine for free refills until my mom finally told us to sit down. Mom and Marc sat there talking. I don't recall what they were saying, but their emotions were flat, they didn't touch each other, and they sat directly across from one another. My mom held her purse on her lap and tightly pulled it into her stomach. She was protecting the only material possession she brought with her from New York.

Marc took us to his family's home where we immediately moved in. We had no suitcases, toys, or belongings. It was just us, the clothes on our bodies, and my mom with her purse. When I was given clean clothes to wear, they weren't new or my own. The clothes were spare clothes from the children who attended the day care inside the home where I'd now reside.

This is where the most haunting childhood memories of my past begin. Together, my brother and I experienced the helpless misery of family dysfunction. We share a lot of the same childhood memories. They are not warm, fuzzy, or plush like a typical child's. They are painful, harsh, cold, physically, and emotionally disturbing, a reality we shared daily until we were separated by calamity.

Who helps us when we are stressed, depressed, living in pain, or dealing with failure? Help is someone who has walked similar paths bearing her deep, dark, and inner true secrets. We gain encouragement and inspiration when we see other people have made it through the same challenges. Life includes a disarray of problems, solutions, the reality of dysfunctional families, personal and marital issues, and unforeseen circumstances. It is easy to act fake, live in hiding, and bury our skeletons from the past. But I refuse to hide my pain. I want to tell all. I have a burning desire within me waiting to be unleashed into this world to help people. I want to help you. I want you to know weeping may come for a night but "joy comes in the morning." (Psalm 30:5)

This is where healing and freedom begin. It's my desire for my story to penetrate hearts with God's love, change lives, break down walls, and give God the glory. Truth matters. Truth makes a difference. And if you allow God to open your eyes and heart to truth in your life, you just may be set free! "And you will know the truth, and the truth will set you free." (John 8:32)

2
The "White House"

We moved into a small, white house surrounded by dirt, rocks, and cactus. The home was excessively cluttered, children ran around all over the place, and darkness consumed every room. The darkness inside was strange since outside was so bright and ruled by the shining sun. The living room curtains always remained closed, and at first, we were seldom allowed out front to play. This helped conceal our presence since we'd just been kidnapped.

Marc introduced us to his family. First I met an older woman with gray hair, missing teeth, and a British accent. Her name was Elizabeth. Elizabeth's husband Tyler stood by in the distance dressed in his military uniform. He was reluctant to speak, and his personality appeared firm and angry. I was never given a personal greeting from that man except a stern glare telling me to stay far away from him and never get in his way.

The last person I met was Marc's younger sister, Natalie. She was in her early twenties, with a stocky appearance, dark hair, and a large mole on her left chin. Natalie seemed friendly and the "normal" one of the family. There was something about her to which I was drawn, and I trusted her because of the happy person she seemed to be. She was playful with me and took me under her wings, giving me attention and love I craved. I began to like Natalie. We bonded right away, forming a friendship. My friendship with her felt like something I had longed for from my own mother. It was odd to feel cared about by someone whom I had just met. At the same time, I continued to feel abandoned by my own mom who was physically present but ignored my existence.

My mom was with me, but she was emotionally distant. She never spoke to me nicely, calmly, or assured me of protection or love. I never felt loved, calmed, or reassured, and I don't remember being hugged by her. There was always a space between us I could never understand. It was painful and it made my heart sad.

Death in the White House

Besides the room my brother and I shared, my mother and her boyfriend shared a bedroom, Elizabeth and her husband a room, and Natalie another. This living arrangement worked well until Elizabeth's husband died. We hadn't lived in the white house long before death made its appearance.

In the middle of the night I was awakened by screaming, crying, and chaos. I heard, "He is bleeding out of his ears." My brother and I jumped up and rushed out of the bedroom. Fear gripped my body, and I stood in the hallway looking around confused, unable to comprehend what was happening.

We were quickly ushered out the front door and into the front yard. We stood barefoot on the rocks in the warm, humid air. The air smelled musky, and the rocks hurt the bottom of my feet. People, mostly strangers, were running in and out of the house. I heard sirens and saw a fire truck, ambulance, and then a helicopter landing in the middle of the street. In the midst of the drama, my brother and I were taken next door to a neighbor and told to lie on their couch and "go back to bed." We kept trying to sneak a view through the curtains, but all we could see were flashing lights. Then there was death.

Elizabeth's husband died from a massive heart attack that night and later was given a full military funeral and burial. For the next week my brother and I were placed in the care of a neighbor two blocks away. We didn't go to the funeral. We were considered too young to attend. This hurt me deeply. It made me feel left out, unimportant, and disconnected to everyone else. I didn't understand why I was left out.

9

Left with no support from the "man of the house," Elizabeth and Natalie were left to fend for themselves babysitting children while my mom, her boyfriend, and we children were "live ins" in a place where we didn't belong and soon to find out- not welcome.

Tyler's death was a turning point in my childhood. Although he didn't have a personal relationship with me, he was the glue holding this already dysfunctional family together with some order and his income. When Tyler had been around, everyone composed themselves and used manners. They treated Tyler and each other with respect and possessed conserved temperaments. No one dared to act ugly or speak above a normal tone. No one dared to laugh or crack a smile. It was obvious Tyler was an intolerant man, and everyone knew it. He had a terrible problem with drinking alcohol and cheating on his wife. It's possible he was feared, rather than respected. Natalie worked at home and helped care for the children. Elizabeth took care of the children, did the cleaning and laundry, and cooked meals.

After Tyler died, our world was turned upside down and shaken. The house became dirty, and things weren't cared for like before. Nothing was thrown out as normal trash; everything was saved and stored. Newspapers were saved and bundled up as well as soda cans and magazines. The house became a home of hoarders. Elizabeth and Natalie babysat more children during the week to compensate for the loss of Tyler's income.

The bedroom my brother and I shared became consumed with kids' clothes, boxes, toys, and newspapers under the bed. The room had a changing table, two cribs, two beds, and one window looking out onto a kids' play area. This was also the room where the children napped. The walls were cold and hard, made of brick and painted yellow. Vintage plastic popcorn art hung on the walls in the design of animals. Snoopy was popular at the time, so he was in a framed picture, too.

The master bedroom was turned into a storage room filled to the top with boxes, and I mean literally to the ceiling. The carport became full of boxes containing junk, no longer able to fit a car. Elizabeth no longer slept in her master bedroom but shared a room and bed with her daughter Natalie. It felt strange to see them lying next to each other sleeping, sharing the same bed, comforter, and intimate space. I didn't understand the reasons for their sleeping arrangement, and I certainly never asked. It was always better to guess at something or choose not to care. Asking questions got me in trouble, and I was quickly put in my place whenever they perceived I was questioning their authority or their reasoning. I was told to mind my own business and to just do what I was told, or else.

The chores and cleaning became neglected, and everyone's attitudes and tones were harsh and angry. This was the new normal.

3
Rejected

While attending kindergarten in New York, I enjoyed playing "Farmer in the Dell" and learning about the Letter People. My favorite thing to do was sit in circle time with all the other kids and do group activities. I loved to hold the large, round crayons in my hand and draw pictures. Although I couldn't draw well, I loved to draw nature, animals, and people. I loved the fresh smell of crayons when I opened the box and the inviting fragrance of smelly markers and scratch n' sniff stickers during art time. Those were the days! Kindergarten was a memorable school year when I had fun and experienced joy as a child.

Then something changed in the people around me, and my circumstances turned grim. If I had to guess at my mother's motives for taking me from my father, I was stolen away and hidden for the selfish purpose of resentment. The weather changed, the scenery changed, and I wasn't around anyone I knew anymore.

First grade in New Mexico wasn't as colorful as my time in New York. Instability and a dysfunctional home created many issues for me and my education. I lived in physical harm with emotional pain and experienced daily anxiety. We were all mistreated and in danger at the white house. The house was quaint from the outside. It was white with green shutters, a one level rambler surrounded by little grass, lots of dirt, and many rocks in the front yard. A banana tree sat outside the front bedroom window and a large tree stood in the front yard.

One of my happy memories was climbing into that big tree. I was so proud of myself for climbing high into the tree. It gave me a feeling of self worth to conquer such a feat. It was a big tree! I sat in the tree and looked around at nature, prairie dogs, and birds. I gained a brief moment of calm I desperately needed and longed for.

Without money or anywhere to go, our options were limited. With some persistent persuasion, Marc talked his mom into letting us stay in her house. But he had to provide rent money, pay utilities, and buy food.

It wasn't long before Natalie, Marc's sister, started revealing her ugly personality. She became aggressive, angry, and violent. Natalie excessively tormented me, my mother, and my brother. She was manipulated and controlled by demonic influence, used as a human agent to destroy us.

While my mom's boyfriend Marc worked during the day, unforeseen circumstances started happening. Bruises on my mom's body were noticed, and too many tears to count came from her eyes. Her eyes were sunken in, and she never smiled, these being signs of the intense pain she was experiencing. As a child I was unable to understand what my mom was going through, but my heart could sense her pain. I somehow believed our circumstances were my fault. A child shouldn't feel responsible for the actions of an adult, but I just couldn't figure out what I did wrong to "make" everything bad happen to us. Somehow, feeling helpless and not being able to make sense out of things made me feel so out of control, I took on more responsibility than I deserved.

This responsibility in itself gave me a false sense of control. I felt guilty all the time. And guilt made me helplessly unable to fix anything! The haunting memories have forever left emotional and physical scars on my body and my mind: the pain, the tears, the fear, the sorrow, the feeling of being alone, and the evil darkness. I remember it all. It was scary, and it was real.

Road Trip

Natalie made me run errands with her because she claimed she was too scared to venture out alone. We went to the grocery store, the gas station, the food bank, and the post office. Our road trips came about two to three times per week. As we drove along in the car, there was often an awkward silence. Sometimes Natalie asked me random questions such as what road we were on or where she needed to turn next. When I said nothing at all or gave any answer, she would pull my hair, slap, or scratch me. This was not a game I could win.

Natalie also used this time for the opportunity to speak badly about my mother and tell me horrible things, like how she didn't love or want me. She called my mother names and told me she couldn't stand her. Natalie once absurdly asked me to think of something sad because she wanted to see me make myself cry. I closed my eyes and thought about someone telling me my mom was dead, and I started crying. Natalie asked me what I was thinking. I told her I thought about my mom dying. She told me how ridiculous I was, and it wouldn't be sad if that happened. Natalie scratched my arm drawing blood and forcefully pulled my hair out for that. She hated my mom and she wanted me to hate her too.

The looks Natalie gave me with her deep, dark brown eyes were chilling. There was a horrifying hatred in her eyes that built up with intensity until it couldn't remain locked inside her anymore. Something indescribable, but as real as this moment, was eating her up inside and killing her spirit, crushing her soul. Ordinary wasn't her style; happy wasn't on her agenda. All she had and all she knew was whoever or whatever tormented her and defined the person she had become. Instead of dealing with her past and pain, she transferred it onto others, looking for a temporary relief never fulfilling her for long. She always needed another fix. She lashed out into another fit of rage and violence, hurting me in order to feed and satisfy her hungry demons.

Natalie took me with her to the airport early one morning to drop someone off. While it was still dark outside on the way home, I fell asleep, leaning my head against the car window in the passenger seat. I was comfortable. Suddenly, Natalie woke me up by slapping me in the face and screaming at me for sleeping. She told me I wasn't allowed to sleep because she was tired, and she needed me to stay awake so I could keep her awake. I apologized tearfully and told her I didn't know. She slapped me more and called me a liar.

Over the years I spent living with Natalie, I was excessively abused by her physically, emotionally, and even sexually. When I started my period at the age of eleven, Natalie was eager to educate me on using tampons. I wasn't excited about them, except to learn in the summer I could still go swimming. She bought a box of tampons and took me into the bathroom showing me how to insert them. She made me lie on the floor naked, forcing me to let her insert them into me. I felt embarrassed and mortified. I was vulnerable and lying there naked while Natalie took over the most personal part of my body. These parts were always covered by clothes, and even as a child, I knew they were supposed to be protected and secret. I didn't speak or ask questions; I stared at the ceiling, feeling cold and yucky. I knew there was nothing I could say or do, because it wouldn't make a difference. I assumed I just didn't matter.

Natalie forced me to show her my private parts on other occasions. She said she needed to look and make sure I didn't have any rashes or anything wrong going on there. She would rub some type of yellow cream on me. Natalie was impressed and obsessed with my breasts and talked about their size and how big they were for my young age.

There was absolutely nothing wrong with me. She made up situations taking advantage of me. I was too scared to tell anyone, and I was confident no one would care or believe me anyway. I was mortified, uncomfortable, and used.

Inside my spirit, I was someone different from whom I saw in the mirror. I didn't know the girl in the mirror. When she looked at me she was just so pathetic. Her blue eyes were always puffy, red and tearful. They stared at me with their own language, saying, "help me." But I was helpless inside, and there was nothing I could do for her. The marks on her body were cruel and demeaning reminders of someone taking over her person in sickening ways. The pain on her face was evident, her mouth rarely able to force a smile. Yet, there was something so beautiful and pure about her youth and innocence which was captivating. Her cheeks were round and delicate with simple and sweet freckles. Freckles also centered on her nose. Her hair was beautiful and glowing blonde, highlighted from the sun. Although her body was beat up and used, she was physically strong. All of these things I could see looking back at me in the mirror. But I still didn't understand who she was, or who I was. We were different, yet connected. I was confused.

Inside my spirit I was energetic, loving, joyful, and wanted to allow my feelings and energy to run free and escape me going forth into a world where it was needed and hopefully wanted. These things inside me which felt right and good were shoved down and never allowed to come out where I lived in darkness and pain. I had to protect myself and stay safe. So, I became a creative mind and found ways to use my imagination. I lived in my own happy place where no one could take away my freedom and joy. In my mind, no one could hurt me. This is where I would dream; this is where I would pretend. I went many places and became many things. One day, I was a teacher with a classroom of students. The next, I was a singer using the garden hose as my microphone. Another day, I owned a hot-dog stand and sold the best and cheapest wieners in town, and on hot summer days I would float for hours in the pool, looking up to the sky trying to find God and imagine heaven. I believed any spaces between the clouds were openings that sucked people in and beamed them up to heaven. If I saw an opening, I would fearfully say, "No to all the openings in the sky until I am one-hundred and three." That was a good number. I wanted to live to be one-hundred and three. As long as I say, "no to all the openings in the sky," I was safe for the day, and I wouldn't die.

I knew my good feelings and thoughts weren't meant to stay locked up inside; they were yearning and bursting to be liberated and make a difference in the world around me. I lived hopeful, believing and waiting to someday be free. Able to just be me and loved for who I was. I planned to someday change the world and make it a better place. I wanted to help people who were hurting just like me. This became a huge realization on May 25th, 1986 as I stood on a highway in my black "pleather" pants, holding hands with hundreds of strangers participating in "Hands Across America." People were there just like me. People who wanted to make a difference, secretly longing for compassion and genuine unity in this world. What if everyone cared, what if everyone wanted to change the world and make it a better place?

When Natalie cooked something I didn't like, I wasn't allowed to refuse it. She literally forced food down my throat. She did this with spinach, broccoli, and cottage cheese. She didn't care how much I gagged or if I threw up.

When Natalie was angry with me, she dug deep and hard into my skin with her fingernails, scratching me and making me bleed. There is more abuse I have locked inside my mind, because it's too tragic to bring to remembrance. As I sit here and write these words, the memories are extremely real. When I allow myself to go back to that time, I remember the pain and events more vividly and in detail. But I can't go back there often and not for long. I won't allow myself to relive that horror. The abuse was devastating for any child to live through or endure. Life shouldn't be like this.

4

The Pain of Abuse

From age five through twelve, I lived through a devastating and painfully abusive childhood. I don't believe a day went by I wasn't abused. No, not even one day! See, that was my prayer: "One day, God, please, just one day is what I want to live without being hit or hurt."

These years were the hardest of my entire life. This pain is what shaped and defined my thinking and caused irrational responses from me, which lingered within far longer than I care to admit. I trusted no one, expected good from no one and anticipated the worst all the time. I had nowhere safe to go, nowhere safe to run. I couldn't even protect myself in a fetal position with my hands and arms covering my face while I was being beaten as an innocent child. The only time I felt safe was when Natalie was sleeping.

Being beaten hurts. It hurt my face on impact and stung for a long time. I remember the stinging and the hot sensation on my cheeks. The red marks went from big welts to just fine lines and sometimes left finger marks. The marks faded over time. No one at school noticed marks or bruises on me. Natalie dressed me carefully to conceal any evidence. My mom, however, knew about the abuse. She not only saw it with her own eyes, but she, too, was slapped around. Natalie pulled her hair and beat her up on numerous occasions. They were two grown women fighting like toddlers. They held onto handfuls of each other's hair and swung each other around the living room on multiple occasions. My mom never started a fight with Natalie; she was always on the defense. My mom was at least Natalie's size and could have taken her. But all she took was the hits that kept on coming.

Natalie also beat on my little brother, but she went after him the least. Maybe the difference was his gender, but regardless it makes no sense like all her other actions. My mom used to take my brother and me into a room and snap pictures of the bruises and marks on us. She threatened to call the police on Natalie, but she never followed through. It hurt emotionally. I didn't understand. I couldn't understand. I knew every day it was coming. It was just a matter of time before Natalie would fly off the handle and come after me for a way to release her rage.

As you continue to read my story, please allow my pain to be used as insight into the world of a hurting child. Because of the horrific abuse I endured and the tragic childhood experiences I lived through, I have acquired beneficial knowledge and beliefs I want to share.

Happy is a Choice

I'm not naïve enough to believe in a perfect, fairy-tale childhood. I understand families have troubles; these things are part of life. Some problems are manageable. These could include a lack of communication in the home causing strife and tension, people not doing their share of chores, a constant bickering and fighting, or rebellious attitudes.

Helpful ways to manage these issues would include effective communication, clearly identifying the problems, and coming up with a plan of agreement by everyone, to take positive action correcting wrong behaviors. The number one challenge is helping people recognize the reality of their problems and assisting them with acceptance. Sometimes counseling is needed and necessary.

When families work together desiring a happy and peaceful home, it's doable and possible. It takes time, energy, and work, but it's worth it. No one ever said life would be easy but there are decisions we can make and actions we can take to help hold our families together. We always have a choice to respond and act in love no matter what is going on around us. We always have the choice to put others before ourselves and live a sacrificial life of giving, loving, and kindness. Sacrifice is putting our own needs and pride behind us and doing what's best for everyone, regardless of how we feel.

Some family troubles are inevitable. This could include a parent being laid off work, a friend or family member dying, divorce, a lack of money, or an event no one has any control over. These things can be extremely stressful and turn lives upside down or threaten to tear you apart. During these times families need to remember God is their number one source, continue in prayer and focus on making their loved ones a priority. We have to stand for what we believe in. We have to fight for what we want. We can't remain passive. We can't give up. There will be battles and trials in life; they are inevitable. It is with hope we wait in expectation. Trust and rely on God to do the impossible trusting that he can bring a positive result from an adverse circumstance. Hope is what we hold onto for the day and take with us into the future. Hope keeps our spirit alive and our heart open to receive anticipated answers from God.

Love is Free

It is the responsibility of parents to provide protection, dignity, basic needs, and emotional support to the indispensable lives of God's prized possessions, our children. "Children are a gift from the Lord; they are a reward from him." (Psalm 127:3)

Children should run and play with a joyful heart and a sense of freedom and enthusiasm in their spirit. They should be loved and encouraged to use and practice their recognizable gifts and talents. Children need to be inspired to pursue their dreams and achieve their goals.

When children are abandoned, neglected, abused, or raised with emptiness in their hearts, there's a void that will eventually need to be filled with something. A child may experience physical or emotional trauma, torment, or pain causing major psychological effects. Some of the effects may not be seen until adulthood. If parents don't fill these voids with what children require, they may later turn to counterfeit products of the world to fulfill their emptiness. For example, if one lacked love or affection, she may seek sexual fulfillment to fill that void. She may use alcohol or drugs to numb the pain of rejection. There are numerous things someone can use or do to attempt to fill a need or try to feel adequate or good enough.

My mother made wrong choices and decisions, putting her and her children in danger and through agonizing hardship. However, I'm also fully aware parents are not always the cause of a child's pain or bad decisions. Adults don't always have problems because of a negative childhood. I'm simply making it clear parents have a significant part in helping a child become a whole and healthy individual. We as parents are given a lot of responsibility, and we're expected to do the best we can with what we have. When it comes down to it, it doesn't matter the amounts of money or resources we have, love is simply free! May we all learn every day to love more and to know better the one who provides love.

"But anyone who does not love does not know God, for God is love." (1 John 4:8)

5

Breaking Out of the White House

Our first move out of the white house was the year I was in second grade. My mom, Marc, my brother, and I moved together into a smaller house. Our new house had one bedroom and was about the size of a college dorm room, not nearly enough space for four of us to live. Walking through the front door was an empty living area with a cold tile floor and one large bed with a plain and bare small window. An old radiator loudly rattled in the corner of the room and a cot lay on the floor for me to sleep on. We didn't have any dressers; all our clothes were kept in boxes. The walls were white with black scuff marks and dirty hand prints on them. There was a small bathroom with a stand up shower, a toilet, and a sink. There was one bedroom with nothing in it except a twin bed and a small TV. Nothing was cozy or warm about that place. It was cold, dirty, and infested with cockroaches. The kitchen was tiny with white metal empty cabinets. There was a small carport with a line of other houses attached. We were now living in, "the projects."

During this time I was happy to be away from Natalie and didn't find myself ducking every time a hand came my way. I was allowed to express myself without fear of being beaten. I had some time to be alone after school which gave me breathing space. My school was conveniently across the street. After school, I let myself in the house with my key.

My afternoons consisted of watching cartoons and playing with my dog until my mom came home. My dog was named Boo, and she was my best friend. Boo was a white and black husky-shepherd mix. Boo listened to me when I talked, she licked my tears away, and she provided me with unconditional love. Boo helped me to calm down and feel better when I was upset and just petting Boo brought me contentment. I loved Boo deeply.

Troubles of their Own

Living with my mom and Marc had its own disadvantages and misery. My mom was manipulative and embarrassing to be around. Her behavior was strange, and she was paranoid of everyone. She frightened me with irrational decisions, crazy actions, and a disorderly temperament. She rarely smiled and was stand-offish to people out in public. My mom spoke negatively, always assumed the worst, and was quick to judge others. You could definitely say she was not a "people person." When we'd go into a store, she would ask me why someone said hi to her or why they smiled at us. She'd say they probably wanted something from her or maybe they were crazy and wanted to hurt us. She made us hurry along out of fear. She didn't like anyone in her personal space; this made her easily agitated and upset. When someone spoke to her, she answered them rudely. She was simply mean to people. My mom didn't have any friends.

Chaotic Living

Communication was difficult for my mom. It consisted of yelling outbursts, arguing, crying, and throwing and breaking anything within her reach. One Christmas, I received a walkman with a cassette tape. It was an expensive gift I had wanted badly that Natalie gave me. I loved listening to my one and only cassette tape of Huey Lewis and The News. Out of rage, my mom smashed my walkman and tape into pieces while she yelled at me and insisted I hurt her feelings with something I said. I don't remember what I may have said and I'm certain it was nothing compared to her allegations. She always heard what she wanted to, and lots of times she made things up.

My mom not only broke my things, but she crushed my heart and made me feel hated. It's completely devastating and painful to be treated this way by your own mother. This is the woman who's supposed to love, care for, and nurture me. This is the woman who's supposed to protect me from the world and stand up for me. All I can do is shake my head and wonder, what was so wrong within her heart and mind to make her act the way she did?

Whenever she hurt me, I cried. Even though I tried, it was hard to hide my tears. I never wanted her to see me cry, because I didn't want to give her the satisfaction of knowing she caused me any pain. She never expressed remorse or offered an apology for anything she did to hurt me or anyone else. Destroying my toys in front of me, she ripped and cut my dolls apart with scissors. My mom stole money from me out my piggy bank and then bashed the bank into the floor. I still remember seeing the pieces of that cute, small, pink pig all over the place. That time I did cry in front of her. I remember the deep aching pain in my heart and the unsettling fear in the pit of my stomach. My mother broke my heart. She caused me emotional distress by her rejection, destructive behaviors and words. Imagine trying to find a greeting card for a mom like that on any given holiday! You can't find one. They all say nice, sweet things; you cringe while reading the cards and just know they are lies. But you pick one out anyway, not wanting to hurt her feelings like she did to you. Funny how forgiveness works.

Not a Gem

My mom had an obsession with jewelry. She stole it, wore it, and collected it. Rings, necklaces, and charms were her favorite, and there was more jewelry in her house than food. When fits of rage would overcome her she would be inclined to pull off her rings and throw them. In anger, she randomly threw her rings out the car window on the highway and on many occasions quite a few went into the thick bushes in front of the projects. She knew very well this childish behavior pushed an automatic anger button in Marc's head and heated up any argument. She was proud of her accomplishment and laughed in his face at his anger, taunting him more.

I never saw Marc physically hurt my mom, but I heard it behind closed doors. The intensity of their fighting was fearsome. It made me cower in apprehension of being injured or seeing my mom hurt by Marc. My brother witnessed Marc tie dog chains around her neck and force her to eat dog food. Strife, anxiety, and constant tension filled the air, and it eventually became the normal expectation for the day when I was with them.

My mom may have been mentally ill and never sought help or treatment. She clearly exhibited signs of various mental illnesses such as bipolar disorder, anxiety disorder, some signs of schizophrenia and depression. I'm not a doctor or a mental health expert who can diagnose, but I am the daughter who had to endure and survive living with a mentally unstable mother.

Broken to Pieces

As a nurse I've worked with mentally ill patients. I've learned signs of suicidal ideations are not always clearly evident. We can't see what's going on inside people's minds. However, people may show signs of suicidal predispositions but have no one to notice or help them.

Around the age of nine years old, I witnessed my mother try to take her life. Mom always took pride in her beauty and in how she did her make-up and hair. She had a special mirror with side lights plugging into the wall. One evening my mom sat on the edge of her bed with her head hanging down. Tears fell from her face and she wept in a loud, hysterical manner. Suddenly, something sprung up in her like she was ignited by hope, but sadly it proved to be anger and hopelessness motivating her actions. She picked up her special mirror, holding onto it tightly, she raised it high and slammed it to the ground, watching it shatter into pieces. Looking down while crying she picked up a sharp piece of glass from the floor and took it to her wrist. She wept as she held onto the glass and cut her wrist. I watched her push the glass in and slowly move it back and forth.

There I was, watching and crying. My mom saw me but my presence didn't matter. I don't remember how deep her cuts were, the amount of blood loss, or who came to help. Maybe my mind blocked the trauma as an internal protective mechanism. I'm thankful she was unsuccessful in attempting to kill herself.

Considering Consequences

Had my mother killed herself, I'd have been unable to comprehend her reasons, intentions and motives. Being so young, her suicide would've left permanent memories, scarring, and guilt pressed deeply into my soul. I'd have been left to forever replay the event in my mind, trying desperately to discover ways to prevent its happening.

Committing suicide leaves so many loved ones behind with unanswered questions, extreme pain, and a life time of void and helplessness. It's helpful for anyone contemplating suicide to understand what their actions can do to the people they leave behind. While suicide may appear an immediate relief from pain and desperation; those left behind have to pick up the pieces without the one they loved there with them. In the deepest, darkest moment of life, without hope or the ability to see light at the end of the tunnel; there is hope. The lies of the enemy work to consume and defeat you, but God is with you. There exists a battle for your soul. God has never left you and he never will. Ultimately, it's up to you to choose life, choose to believe God and allow him to embrace you with his love, and trust him to help you. He will supply all your needs; he will give you a perfect peace that surpasses all understanding. When you give up and surrender, waving your white flag in the air; surrender yourself completely to Jesus. The enemy's way is death; God's way is life. "The thief's purpose is to steal and kill and destroy. My purpose is to give them a rich and satisfying life." (John 10:10)

Truth be Told

There is something you need to hear and know. You are a child of God. You are truly loved. Even if you feel lonely, you are never alone. God is there and always with you. He will never leave you or forsake you. He is there for the reaching, but often times we don't get close enough to hear or see him. We must press into God and never give up. Just because we don't see our prayers answered immediately does NOT mean they won't be answered at all. Faith believes God is doing something no matter what we see or feel. "Faith is the confidence that what we hope for will actually happen; it gives us assurance about things we cannot see." (Hebrews 11:1) Having faith can also be said as having confidence. Have confidence in God and know He can do anything. He is bigger than anything that comes our way and everything we face. God is for us and not against us! "So be strong and courageous! Don't be afraid and don't panic before them. For the Lord your God will personally go ahead of you. He will neither fail you nor abandon you." (Deuteronomy 31:6)

Important Note: If you feel depressed or so desperate that death seems the only way out, don't believe that lie. There are people who love you. There is help and hope. Take the step to reach out to someone you trust with your thoughts and feelings and please get professional help and support. You can also go to http://www.suicidepreventionlifeline. org/ or call The National Suicide Prevention Lifeline at 1-800-273-8255.

6
Realities of Poverty

My mom never had a license or even a desire to drive a car, so we rode the city bus or walked.

The mall was the most frequent place my mom would take me. Our trips to the mall were interesting. Mom had incredible skill at shoplifting. She was subtle and clever at her craft. I kept myself at a distance while watching her look at jewelry with intense interest. She calmly looked around before putting things in her purse or pocket. She wore lots of jewelry and had plenty in her large jewelry box at home. Sometimes she and Marc hocked the jewelry at pawn shops for cash.

My mom also stole cigarettes for Marc, and food from the grocery store. She and Marc filled up grocery carts with items, pushed it out the door, and then unloaded it in their car without paying. I felt a sense of shame and embarrassment witnessing these things. There is something inside our human minds alerting us and awakening our conscience, making us aware of right and wrong. Was their conscience impaired or did they ignore it? I never told her I knew what was going on or asked any questions. She would've yelled at me, denied it all, and called me a liar. My mom was good at manipulating people and even making herself believe her own lies. The moment a lie escaped her lips, there was no way to make her admit the truth. Her lies became her truth.

All I had was Hope

While living in the projects, clothes were rags, toys were things used from the kitchen, and food was scarce. I had a couple Barbie dolls with only the clothes on their bodies. Since neither Christmas nor birthdays produced the huge Barbie doll house, cars, or furniture to go with it, I settled for my own creative ideas and made do with things lying around. My most loved accessory was a waterbed I created for my Barbie. I couldn't wait until a bread bag was emptied, because I took them and filled them up with water, then tied the end with a rubber band. I loved my Barbie's waterbed even though it sprang frequent leaks.

Food wasn't taken for granted. Peanut butter and graham crackers were the two things filling our bare cupboard most. I noticed it was also the same snack at my mom's workplace for the preschool kids. She worked as a preschool teacher, and Marc worked on cars. It wasn't a big secret we had things in our home that were stolen. She often pulled toilet paper rolls, plastic bags, and other things out of her purse she'd taken from her workplace to help provide for our family. Although my mom and Marc had jobs, they were still broke and unable to provide well for my brother and me.

Living in this unstable and dirty environment made me feel anxious, scared, and stressed. I never knew how to relax, because my body and mind were living in a constant "fight or flight" response. I was unable to enjoy life or have fun because I didn't feel safe or that I deserved anything good. My mother was always telling me how horrible I was and never proved to love me.

Presently, I'm not feeling sorry for myself. However, I feel sorry for the child within me that was hurting so badly, wounded so deeply, and so lost within during childhood. I didn't experience the life a child deserves. I wasn't asking or looking for much, just some love, approval, and protection. I didn't want the newest gadget off the internet or a new wardrobe. I knew better than to ever ask for a toy or something new. I was well aware we had no money. I just wanted to feel and be loved and secure. I carried a deep, lonely, and empty feeling never filled by a parent's love.

I accept I can do nothing about my past, and I choose not to wallow in despair. I choose to use what has happened and allow God to grow me and use it for good by helping others. I accept my past.

I want the world to know Jesus snatched me from the enemy's hand. He delivered me from hopelessness and despair. I was sinking in an ocean full of despondency. My heart was desperate and broken. I wanted love so desperately. I was a daughter never approved, loved, or accepted until I discovered my true Father, the one seated in heaven, my creator. My heavenly Father gave me all the strength I needed and filled me with an unexplainable hope. This feeling inside of me motivated me to keep on keeping on, no matter what my circumstances looked like and no matter how I felt. There was an invisible hand that carried me, an invisible love that held me, and an invisible joy that filled me. While I had no one to live for and nothing to look forward to, I kept pressing on and moving forward in life. I can't explain it, but I know, "hope kept me alive."

Hope is the key that unlocks the door for our future. Hope keeps our passion, energy, and existence in motion. Without hope many dreams have been surrendered, marriages have been destroyed, relationships have been damaged, and lives have been drastically changed or taken at a high cost. If you have nothing else, you do have hope. If you don't know what hope is or what hope feels like, his name is Jesus.

7

My Fatherly Influence

Marc was around five foot eight. He had a large pot belly, black hair, an unkempt beard, and tattoos on his arms. He possessed vile secrets in his heart. Marc was a repulsive child molester, woman beater, and drug user: a criminal. His attire consisted of mainly white T-shirts stained with dirt and oil, his bottoms were dirty, saggy jeans. In his spare time he worked on his own car under the carport. He worked all days and hours of the week as a mechanic.

Being alone with Marc made me incredibly uncomfortable. One dark night while he sat on the couch, he pulled down his pants and asked me to do something sexual with him, while my mom slept in the other room. His eyes peered at me with a blank and evil stare after he had just smoked a joint. Scared and helpless, I quickly said, "No," and left the room. There were many times Marc would have taken advantage of my innocence and youth had I not been shielded by the protective hand of God.

Some nights it was hard to sleep as I heard my mom and Marc in the next room. My mom constantly yelled "No," and she kept saying, "You're hurting me." I could hear awful and embarrassing words and noises. The sounds echoed in the room like she was being raped. I can't imagine the pain and torment he put my mom through. I just lay there unable to run, unable to help, hearing every word and every sound. I cuddled my white stuffed rabbit named Jack and eventually drifted into an exhausted sleep.

31

Marc smoked marijuana frequently. He had small pipes and roach clips all around the house in plain sight. He also carried paraphernalia in his car and in his pocket. Bags of weed sat around the house or in the glove compartment of his red, rusty 1976 Ford Cougar. He never had the decency to hide any of it. When his pipe was lit up, the hideous odor of marijuana was enough to make me vomit.

Rejections Reality

No child should ever have to face this heart breaking life event I experienced: my mother gave me away. Rejection and abandonment were now permanent on my resume of life experiences. When I was seven years old, she handed me over to live with Elizabeth and Natalie. They became my new caretakers. My mother didn't like or trust these women and had been beaten many times before by Natalie. She even knew we, her own children, were physically harmed by Natalie. I still can't fathom how she came to the drastic decision to give me to them, knowing what kind of life I was going to endure. I've often asked myself, "What kind of mindset did she possess to do something like that as a parent? Did she experience any pain and agony with her choice? Was it desperation? Did she believe in her own mind it was best for me?"

Unanswered questions remain. Why would Elizabeth and Natalie want me living in their home again? Or why was I given away and my brother was not? I've spent a lot of time and energy trying to figure out answers to many questions I simply don't understand. I've accepted some of my questions on this earth may never be answered here. The reality is some things we just can't understand.

Natalie drove onto our dirt road in her baby blue 1976 Volare. I heard her coming with the sound of the rocks crunching under her tires. She picked me up and I went with her, taking a small bag of clothes and a couple stuffed animals. Driving away, to live again in the white house, I was so confused. I didn't know what place was better to live. I didn't understand all the circumstances going on around me. The saddest and hardest part was saying good-bye to Boo. I had promised her I'd never leave her. The only happy thoughts I had about going back to live in the white house were, attending cleaner schools and having nicer teachers. Elizabeth and Natalie also had a few dogs, rabbits, two ducks, and a cat. And in their backyard stood, a four-foot deep, above-ground swimming pool. Those were the highlights.

Swim or Die

The heat in New Mexico almost made it essential to have a pool just to make summers bearable. The pool was lots of fun unless I was being held under the water, thrown around, or splashed by ruthless and ignorant adults who knew I couldn't swim. They didn't care though; I was their rag doll entertainment in the pool. Fearful of going under the water and drowning, I never went under without plugging my nose. The first time I tried to swim getting water in my nose and down my throat; I came up choking and gasping for air. That was enough to scare me to death. And the last time I attempted swimming under the water. No one helped or encouraged me, so I just swam my own way doggie paddling.

There was nothing professional or chemically safe about the pool. In fact, it was drained and refilled frequently. The pump rarely worked, and after it broke, it was never replaced. It didn't take long for the water to turn green and slimy, which meant the lining of the pool was full of algae, bacteria, bugs, and disgusting smells. They tried "shocking" the water with chemicals from the store, but that lasted a short while or didn't work at all. In time, the pool was drained and the "pool boy" went in with bare feet, a bucket, rags, scrubber brushes, and bleach.

(The pool boy was me.) They watched me and instructed what to do. Stroke by stroke, bottles of bleach later, and a couple days after cleaning the lining and rinsing it down, the pool was as clean as it was getting. My body hurt, my feet smelled and hurt from the bleach, but the pool was clean. It was rinsed down and filled back up, ready for a new start. This routine occurred a few times each summer.

8
Living with the Enemy

Mental illness and pure evil itself can claim their roles in giving a person sadistic ideas and terrifying temperaments, causing them to commit outrageous acts of violence. I'll never know what Natalie's past experiences were, what kind of pain she carried, or exactly why she abused me. I only know and live with deep internal wounds caused by the consequences of her choices and her outrageous behavior.

Natalie bounced around in the working world and never held one job for long. She cleaned doctor's offices, worked at Taco Bell, drove an ice cream truck, and had several other employment turnovers. She didn't date nor have many friends. She spent most of her time at home with her mom and had one girl friend. She dressed in plain, older women's clothing, didn't wear make-up, and was obese. Natalie would show an occasional smile and appeared to be friendly in front of people, but when the sun went down, she became something shocking. She was a demonic monster lurking in the white house waiting to erupt like vomit being spewed out in a horror film. She was erratic, and with her there was never a moment of certainty.

Natalie constantly argued and fought with her own mother. Her actions and words were indecent, showing no respect towards anyone. She spent hours talking on a beige phone connected to the kitchen wall with a long, raveled cord. When her mom needed her or suggested she get off the phone, she would throw the phone at her mom in anger and try to hit her with it. Sometimes they chose to throw their shoes at each other, mainly flip-flops. Elizabeth and Natalie argued often over where they would get money to pay the bills. Elizabeth cried because she missed her husband. She accused Natalie of not helping and reprimanded her for not being supportive. Natalie ignored her mom, left the room, or yelled at her and made her cry more. Many times they accused each other of not caring about the other, which was in fact how it appeared.

Over Controlling

Natalie only allowed me to visit with my mom on special occasions. I saw my mom once in awhile on weekends and on holidays such as Christmas or Easter. Natalie spoke nastily about my mom and made me believe horrible things. She told me my mom gave me up because she never loved me or wanted me and my mom had abortions because she couldn't afford any more children. Natalie became more controlling the longer I lived with her. Her words were deranged, and her intentions unclear. Natalie did everything in her evil power to make life as miserable as possible for me.

Living with Elizabeth and Natalie was a constant nightmare. I walked on eggshells, endured physical pain, cried many tears, but the worst pain was not being able to understand why I was mistreated. I knew I was different from other children my age. Just seeing them have better lives and decent families made my pain worse. I saw they were happy, loved, and taken care of. Other children carried themselves differently than I did. They looked secure in knowing who they were and where they came from. They smiled and laughed in a free-style way. They weren't afraid to have fun. They didn't walk around with their heads hung low, living in fear. They wore nice clothes and shoes without holes. Their clothes were clean and stylish. On special occasions at school I was unable to sign up for parties or bring goodies because of our lack of money. The other kids had the neatest bikes, skateboards, and roller skates. Inside I was envious, jealous, and feeling left out. In the first grade I stole a small toy from another kid out of his desk because I didn't think it was fair he had one and I didn't. I, too, wanted what he had.

The other girls were pretty. They wore accessories and jewelry. They had cute little purses and bags. They looked so nice while I looked and was dressed like a "tomboy." I noticed other kids looked at me strangely and intentionally stayed away from me like I was a plague. They didn't want to talk to me or play with me at school. On the playground I hung from the monkey bars alone. No one pushed me on the swing, and I wasn't invited over, even when we played Red Rover. I sat alone during lunch time at my own table as a total outcast. When I asked to sit with a group, they laughed at me and said no. This hurt my innermost being and my pain made me want to crawl in a hole and hide from the world. Rejection has no mercy. This agonizing pain went on for years. I honestly remember more than I'd like to and wish there was an eraser for my tormenting thoughts.

Bizarre Behavior

At a young age, I was taught how to steal. I stole bikes, skateboards, and toys from people's yards at night. We went on car rides around surrounding neighborhoods, hunting for easy targets. Most things were thrown immediately in the trunk, and we drove off nonchalantly. There were times Natalie and Elizabeth went so far as to make me ride bikes we stole back to the white house. I rode the bikes home alone and was always afraid of getting caught, in trouble, or lost in the dark night. They kept the toys we stole and used them for the day care, storing them in their backyard or under the carport.

We continually lacked money when I was growing up. We constantly fought the fight of living in poverty. Elizabeth and Natalie used me to help them survive by teaching and making me steal money. We spent many days and hours coaxing money from people. Natalie drove me around various neighborhoods and made me walk door-to-door asking for money. I wore a special T-shirt Natalie had made with false logos printed on them. When someone answered their door I'd say, "Hi, my name is Debbie," (or whatever fake name I was using for the day) "and I'm collecting money for the Cancer Society, would you like to give?" People would give willingly and generously to different groups, causes, and organizations which I pretended to represent. The money was collected in an envelope or a container. I walked long hours in the hot desert sun exhausted while I was forced to lie. Sometimes after a long day we would go for dinner or pie, and sometimes it was just enough money to keep on the hot water.

Because we lived in poverty, the state of New Mexico helped take care of us. We used food stamps to buy groceries, and our medical and dental care was provided by the county. We received food from the food bank, and I remember driving to a warehouse for large blocks of cheese which made tasty cheese crisps for meals. Our clothes were hand-me-downs from Goodwill or yard sales. The gas fueling the car was sometimes paid for, but other times, Natalie fueled up and drove away without paying.

Natalie mail-ordered items from catalogs and made me go out and sell stuff door-to-door. The items consisted of things like Light-sabers, stuffed animals, small toys, key chains, candy bars, cotton candy, and snacks. She would send me out with a box full of items I could physically carry. People bought stuff from me as I stood on their front door step as a child sales representative. I was also dropped off at stores and told to ask people for money when they walked out. I stood at the front doors with a can or an envelope and again begged for money. People unknowingly, but generously; put their hard earned cash into the hands of a child who worked for immoral crooks.

The Lying Game

Water fountains are beautiful. It's mesmerizing and calming to just stand still in front of a large fountain and watch the water fall. It falls in so many patterns and the sound can carry me to the ocean, giving me a sense of serenity.

How many times have you thrown coins into a fountain and wished for something magical? As kids, my brother and I were occasionally given some pennies to throw into the fountains at the mall. This made us happy to anticipate our wishes coming true. However, our true intention was to steal from the fountain. My brother and I were taken to the mall together and instructed to "pretend fight" or play around the fountain and either fall in or push each other in. We grabbed as many coins as we could and stuffed them into our pockets and pants. Sometimes the first "act" wasn't enough, so we'd find another fountain for a reenactment. Alas, we then had money in the form of stolen coins to use for food that evening. Hopefully, someone before us had wished to help feed the poor. - Than that coin met its intention.

Fast and Free

Lying comes naturally to help us defend and protect ourselves. But I also learned lying can be mastered with skill after practice. I was taught to lie as if being trained for professional acting. My part was to say a few lines to scheme people out of food. We drove around to various fast food restaurants, and I ran inside telling the cashier we'd just gone through the drive thru and something was missing from our bag. The cashier would apologize and give me whatever item I denied receiving. I left with a free burger, fry, or drink and a smile! We deceived several drive-thrus in one evening into providing us with sufficient food for that night.

Restaurants were also an easy target for the lying game. Restaurants as a business were eager to please their customers; even more so, they were always quick to calm down the irate ones. After a meal, when it came time to pay the bill, one of the adults would complain about the service or the food. Sometimes they planted one of their own hairs in the food for added drama. They demanded to speak to a manager and after arguing and complaining, the meal was on the house. I suppose when there is no money and times are tough, desperation causes people to do different and outrageous acts to help them survive. For me and my family, this was our way of life.

Basic Needs

I've never traveled to a poverty stricken country or gone on a mission trip to experience for myself their devastation lived out on a daily basis. I can't imagine having life without clean water to drink, going days without food, or living in sickness and disease without medical care. This isn't something we think about all the time, but it's something worth taking time to think over.

Pause for a moment and consider some daily amenities we have readily available compared to third world countries: electricity, medical and dental care, and safe housing. Smaller items we use daily but rarely consider include shoes, deodorant, and tooth brushes with toothpaste. Then there is the never ending list of things we enjoy daily other countries aren't able to experience, considering they don't even have their "basic" needs met: cell phones, computers, televisions, or how about a fresh cup of coffee each day!

We live here in an astounding country called the United States of America. Freedom, liberty, opportunity, and rights are the language we speak and the blessed life we live. We don't need to feel condemned or guilty for our prosperous lives but only inspired to look at how we are using our blessings. Are we living to glorify God, or are we living to glorify ourselves?

Lacking Amenity

New Mexico is not a third world country, however, even in New Mexico after the sun goes down, it gets cold. There were plenty of cold, dark nights without electricity. The utility man not only came by to check our meter but to shut off our service. It distressed me when the hot water was shut off. Thankfully, we had a gas stove assisting with our baths. Large kettles of water were boiled and dumped into the tub for bathing. I helped carry the large black kettles back and forth from the bathroom to the stove. The water usually cooled off fast so there was no time for play in the tub, and everyone used the same bath water which ended up cold and brown.

Living in poverty feels like being empty inside. Negative feelings and thoughts shout, "I'm worthless and life is hopeless. Nobody cares about me, and that's why I have nothing." I know what it's like to feel hungry but have nothing to eat, to open up a fridge and see it bare, and to open a cupboard to no food. It didn't make any sense to me that we had no food in our home. All I could do was listen to my feelings and believe what they said, "I was worthless so I deserved nothing."

I will never forget where I came from. I won't take for granted that God saved me from despair. I'm forever grateful for God's great mercy as he's done so much for me and given me a life full of grace, things beyond what I deserve. I want God to use me to bless others who have even less than I did. I give to others in need not because I have too much, but because I know what it's like to not have.

Selfless Love

What I've learned from my poverty stricken days is everything in this world is God's. We can't go shopping and put a single thing in our cart that's not His. God provides our jobs and therefore the money we make to buy what we need. Things we own and use are borrowed from God and we can't take them with us when we die. This is an insightful epiphany when we allow it to connect from our minds to our hearts! When we tithe, give offerings, or sacrifice our money and possessions, we are giving back to God what is His in the first place. When we give to others we will be greatly blessed and discover it's impossible to "out-give" God!

There are many opportunities where God can use us to be a blessing to someone. It may be in tithing, helping out a friend or neighbor, sponsoring a child from another country, or in other unique ways. The joy of giving is in essence one of the most rewarding acts of selfless love.

"If someone has enough money to live well and sees a brother or sister in need but shows no compassion--how can God's love be in that person? Dear children, let's not merely say that we love each other; let us show the truth by our actions." (1 John 3: 17-18)

Mission Zone

The world is a mission zone where we can live with purpose to reach lost and hurting people. We are called to serve, give, and sow God's love and resources. We can't stay comfortable and cozy expecting people to come to us.

"For you have been called to live in freedom, my brothers and sisters. But don't use your freedom to satisfy your sinful nature. Instead, use your freedom to serve one another in love." (Galatians 5:13)

Let's ask ourselves, who are we feeding? Who are we reaching out to? Who are we judging because we don't understand what it's like to feel dirty, alone, lost, or broken? Who are we looking down upon because we don't remember what it's like to not trust anyone? Who are we giving food, drink, and clothes to because we know what it's like to be in need? "And the King will say, 'I tell you the truth, when you did it to one of the least of these my brothers and sisters, you were doing it to me!" (Matthew 25:40)

Let us embrace each other with a warm heart and attitude. So many people out there just need a word of encouragement. Remember when someone took your hand and helped you out before? It's time for our hearts to beat together as one with Christ and go forth into the world with a bigger intention to make a difference. It's time to be the eyes of Jesus and grasp opportunities we see, to help and fervently serve others in our daily reach. We don't need to search far. We have friends, neighbors, teachers, cashiers, co-workers, and yes, even people from church we can help.

If we pray and ask God to show us people with needs to meet, He won't disappoint. God will speak to us and guide us in all our ways. Don't be concerned about what others think or say, just be obedient. It's time to move out of our comfort zone and into the mission zone. Who can you reach today?

9
Amazing Grace

When I was in first grade, a family in our neighborhood invited me to church with their kids. A church bus picked us up on Sunday mornings on the street corner. The bus was an old school bus named "The Joy Bus." It was painted colorfully with the church's name on the sides. I stood enthusiastically waiting, each Sunday morning on the street corner, ready to get picked up. The bus seats were warm, soft, and bouncy. I rode along bouncing up and down looking out the window to a world of sunshine and freedom. We sang fun worship songs and played games on our ride to and from church. Once we arrived at church we were ushered into our own place just for us kids. It was incredibly fun to dance, sing, watch skits, eat, and learn about God. Going to church made me happy, and I was comforted by the love and peacefulness I experienced.

I clearly remember sitting in a small group setting on the floor in a circle with other children. We were listening to the teacher talk about Jesus while she used pictures of Him on a felt board to explain a story. After the lesson the teacher asked if anyone wanted to ask Jesus into their hearts. I immediately raised my hand and asked Jesus in my heart believing and knowing with everything in me, "He was real." I can't explain the faith I had; I just believed! Jesus and I have had a relationship ever since. The Bible says Jesus loves us so much that He gave his life for us. This is truth and proof of His amazing grace and love; "We know what real love is because Jesus gave up his life for us." (1 John 3:16)

Throughout my childhood, God kept his hand upon me, and he grew me in a relationship with Him. It amazes me when I look back to see all the times he drew me close and helped me. Even after the church bus era, neighbors would invite me and take me with their family to church. I'd often go to Vacation Bible School and attend other events in the Christian churches. I was drawn to the astounding love and promises of God and clung to the hope he provided. God constantly sent people into my life to minister to me and lead me closer to him.

In Church I learned to pray and talk to God. I learned worship song lyrics I still carry in my heart today. In prayer, I questioned God and asked him why I had to live through daily pain and why I had to hurt so much.

There were many times I questioned God and his reality. I wanted Him to prove Himself to me. I asked Him to play with me. I'd throw a ball or rock across the yard, just waiting for Him to pick it up and throw it back. When the object wouldn't come back to me, I didn't give up; I chose not to doubt. I still had faith and hope inside and believed no matter what, He was real.

When I was sick, I prayed and believed God for healing. I received prayer through the radio as I laid my hand upon it and listened to the preacher pray for any sickness and disease to leave my body. Playing outside I fell on a wooden fence getting splinters all over my body. I lay in a bath tub crying out to God for help. Natalie came in and laughed when she heard me, but I know God heard and helped me.

I'm so thankful I never gave up hope as a child and God never gave up on me. God went on to prove his faithfulness to me in more ways than I can count or ever deserved.

Trust is Essential

One important thing we must learn to do is trust. Trust God is always working on our behalf. Just because we don't see our prayers answered immediately does not mean they won't be answered. When we don't see God doing what we want, He may have better plans. Trust that God is doing something no matter what you see. This is called faith.

"And it is impossible to please God without faith. Anyone who wants to come to him must believe that God exists and that he rewards those who sincerely seek him." (Hebrews 11:6)

It's extremely difficult to trust God when you don't know what to expect in life. It's hard to trust God when your past is full of failures, disappointments, and pain. However, I will tell you from experience, when you do start trusting God, you will be filled with a peace surpassing all understanding, your faith will increase, and it opens the door for God to work in your heart and life to do mighty works. How do I know? Because I've been on both sides of the bridge! One side doubts, and the other side trusts. It's not easy, but it's worth crossing over to the better side.

Don't just listen to what I have to say, but listen and believe in the eternal and powerful word of God. "Trust in the Lord with all your heart; don't depend on your own understanding. Seek His will in all you do, and He will show you which path to take. Don't be impressed with your own wisdom. Instead, fear the Lord and turn away from evil. Then you will have healing for your body and strength for your bones." (Proverbs 3:5-8)

10
Bullied

All the normal girls went shopping and had fun choosing and trying on outfits. That was not me, because I wasn't normal (or so I thought). Natalie dressed me and gave me no choice in what to wear. She chose my outfits from my cardboard box dresser. I had outfits that looked like Orphan Annie's and some shirts making me look like a sailor. My clothes were ridiculous. Some were adult fashioned and over-sized, ripped, and stained. Many times I had to wear the same things over. I wasn't dressed like everyone else. This made it more obvious I didn't come from a normal family. Because of this, I was bullied and made fun of by the kids in school.

The only part of me Natalie cared for was my hair. She styled my hair in all different ways. I wore pig tails and small barrettes; she gave me perms and sometimes put in chemicals to straighten my hair. She curled my hair with a curling iron and gave me haircuts. Natalie liked to take time to do my hair after she had beaten me. This sadistic behavior was her way of showing some remorse for what did to me. She was sick and controlling with a twisted mind, void of reasoning.

Word Games

People say words can't hurt us, but we know that's not true. People use mean and nasty words for the very purpose of trying to hurt each other. My favorite phrase when I was young was, "I'm rubber and you're glue, whatever you say bounces off me and sticks back on you."

It was magical to me because I believed if I said it, my pain would hurt less or the names wouldn't be true. I experienced a lot of name calling from kids at school, from kids in our neighborhood, and from Natalie and Elizabeth.

The names hurting me most were the ones I was called from the people in my life who were supposed to be taking care of me. I was hatefully called a "tramp," "hot to trot," "lazy," "worthless," "crazy like your mom," "no good," and even a "little bitch." All these names were lies. Their name calling was all a ploy from the devil planting those things in my mind and trying to make me believe it. The devil had a plan to destroy me, and he used Natalie and Elizabeth as accomplices. There is a constant battle for our souls. The enemy wants nothing more than to defeat and render us helpless. We need to be mindful of his ploys. "The thief's purpose is to steal and kill and destroy. My purpose is to give them a rich and satisfying life." (John 10:10)

Make Believe or Not?

Name calling can hurt children for a lifetime, setting them up for a constant battle of low self-esteem. Spoken words can become a person's reality and affect the way they view or perceive themselves. As a parent, teacher, or any authority figure in someone's life, we are held responsible, and we need to be cautious of the words we choose to use for or against someone. Words are powerful weapons and can be used to build up or destroy. I've suffered immensely from verbal abuse. I've battled low self-esteem and paranoia. I believed I wasn't loved or cared about. I felt I was worth nothing, and I know if I had been spoken to better, I wouldn't have struggled so severely with low self esteem. Words of hatred and evil were planted inside my mind as a child. These bad names and words were seeds which were watered constantly with negativity as I was growing up. The seeds reaped a large harvest of negative and abnormal thoughts and emotions. They became my identity and my reality.

To defeat the lies of the enemy, I've been down a long road of recovery in discovering who I am in Christ. Discovering what God says about us in His word and knowing the truth of His love will oppose the lies we've been told. It is the truth that sets us free! (John 8:32) I'm thankful God's love and his word has the power to renew my mind.

God has healed and delivered me from the damaging lies of my childhood. "But we are a chosen people, a royal priesthood, a holy nation, God's special possession, that you may declare the praises of him who called you out of darkness into his wonderful light." (1 Peter 2:9 NIV)

No More Bull

Due to my dysfunctional childhood, I attended ten different schools from Kindergarten through eighth grade and I was always the "new kid." I never won a popularity contest in school. I simply had no friends. Some kids spitefully called me hurtful names and relentlessly taunted me for a good laugh.

There were plenty of bullies around. I was bullied in school, at the bus stop, and even in the neighborhood. I succumbed to physical fights and was hurt by others while also disgracefully hurting them. I never threw the first punch, but I didn't hesitate to fight back. During school lunches I sat alone feeling ashamed, hurt, and embarrassed. I was emotionally depressed, enduring pain caused by others who chose to humiliate me. I wonder if they were trying to reflect their own insecurity and pain onto me. Did they receive a secret sense of gratification from laughing and teasing me? Was I the most vulnerable scapegoat? They should have just been thankful they didn't have to be me.

Being bullied made me feel unaccepted, rejected, alone and unworthy of any good thing. If I couldn't be accepted by my own peers, why should I bother trusting anyone? Shouldn't they be the ones who are compassionate and able to understand me? In reality, we were one of the same. I walked around with my head hung low and cried many tears. I ran out of class rooms sobbing with pain in the middle of my chest from panic and anxiety after being humiliated by classmates. I was made fun of for having crooked teeth, for being fat, and I was called "pizza face" because of acne. My lips and butt were made fun of for being big, and I was called derogatory names, including the most offensive word in English. The pain in my heart hurt so deep. I wanted to run far and never face those kids again. I had no help and no love to go home to. I faced it all alone and wanted help so desperately, but no one ever came to my rescue.

I tried my best to hide my pain by acting like the class clown. I discovered acting silly and dumb gave them all a reason to laugh and point at me. This felt better because it was self inflicted instead of random, intentional rejection. I tried opening up and sharing my feelings in the hope my pain would touch their hearts and encourage them to care, but it only fueled their relentless taunting. It seemed regardless of how hard I tried to defend myself or prepare myself for the bullying, the pain was always unbearable.

I share my hurt and my heart with you for this reason: If I didn't have the love and hope of Jesus, I'd have taken my own life. That is how profound, deep, and disturbing the pain was.

Someone reading this has been, is being, or knows someone who's being bullied. We can no longer just stand by and watch hearts and lives become destroyed by bullying. It is selfish, disrespectful, persistent, and ugly.

Call it whatever you want: bullying, teasing, name calling, taunting, provoking, or threatening. I call it cowardly, sickening, insecure, and selfish behavior resulting in torment. This behavior must not be tolerated! We have to support each other and come together to stop bullying.

If you are being bullied; please tell someone and get help. Don't assume someone knows what's going on and will come to you. And just as well, don't assume someone sees and knows, but refuses to help. Don't let fear keep you from walking in the freedom you deserve. Talk to a parent, teacher, trusted friend, family member or someone from church. No one should have to live in constant torment. Kids are committing suicide because of bullying. Trust me; the brokenness bullying causes takes a long time to heal. You may be saving someone's life or even you own. Be brave and speak up. You have the courage within you. You are stronger than you think.

If you are the one bullying or putting someone else through this turmoil, stop it! One moment of making a joke out of someone can cause long term pain. This is a serious matter. Also consider yourself. You may be upset or hurting inside and you don't realize the pain you are causing others. It is okay to talk about this. Find someone you can trust to help you!

What helped me through my pain, more than anything else is, Jesus. Although no person came to my rescue, God was there to comfort me and give me courage to keep on going every day.

Pray and ask God for whatever you need and expect him to help you. He loves you more than you know. You can always count on Him to wipe your tears, heal your pain, and help you in every situation. Don't try to do life alone! Life is better when we journey with Jesus.

"And I am convinced that nothing can ever separate us from God's love. Neither death nor life, neither angels nor demons, neither our fears for today nor our worries about tomorrow—not even the powers of hell can separate us from God's love." (Romans 8:38)

11
Cold Steel Bars

ou can observe prisons in movies, TV shows, and documentaries. But nothing beats the reality of being inside a prison. My brother and I experienced the inside of a prison when we were young; witnessing the frightening, cold, and stale dungeon. Our mom's boyfriend Marc was charged, found guilty, and incarcerated for using and dealing drugs, and for the molestation of a child.

My mom took us with her to visit Marc. The woman at the front desk signed us in, and we waited for the guard to take us back. We walked down a long hallway coming to an enclosed area with no windows where there were more guards. We stepped in the doors to visiting area, and were greeted by cold air, a musky smell, sounds of steel crashing, and guards with guns. I saw Marc through a thick glass. Handcuffs wrapped around his ankles limiting his steps as he walked, and his hands were handcuffed in front of him. He was wearing a bright orange jump suit and tears ran down his face falling into his scruffy beard. My mom talked to Marc on a phone while looking at him through a glass window. I stood close and listened as he begged my mom not to leave him apologizing for things he'd done. His voice was weak and shaky and his eyes were gloomy. Marc didn't look like his big strong intimidating self; he looked worried and uncertain. My mom angrily agreed to wait for him until he was released. She cried and yelled at him over the phone. --What an example of "hopeless abandon." I didn't understand her reasoning for staying with him.

This would have been the perfect opportunity to get away. Whether she stayed with him out of love, fear, or nowhere to go is a mystery to me.

Without means to pay rent or survive on her own, my mom packed her things and moved back into the white house with Natalie, Elizabeth, and my brother and me until Marc was released from jail. This time was extra stressful for everyone. Natalie and my mom argued and physically fought. They pulled each other's hair. Natalie once scratched my mom down her face with a fork during an intense argument. My mom succumbed to Natalie's abuse in fear of being kicked out and made homeless.

Act of Betrayal

Natalie hated my mother. I know this because Natalie told me all the time. She harbored perverted jealousy, rage, and wicked feelings towards her. The evil thoughts Natalie entertained caused her to use me to humiliate and violate my own mother.

My mom had beautiful, long blonde hair many women envied. She took great care of her hair, cherished it, and brushed it twice daily. One night while my mom slept soundly, Natalie gave me a pair of large, sharp scissors and told me to go into my mom's room and cut off some of her hair. Reluctantly obedient, I did it. Quietly, I tiptoed into the bedroom, sneaking behind my mom while she lay innocently asleep; I grabbed a chunk of her hair, and cut it off. I quickly ran out of the room and back to Natalie with the scissors and my mom's hair in my hand. Natalie was disgustingly appreciative as shown by the sick smile on her face and her haunting laugh. I was shocked with myself that I was able to do something so mean and vindictive.

The next morning, my mom woke up screaming in her room, crying about her hair. She asked everyone who did it and was unsuccessful in obtaining a confession. My mom accused Natalie. Natalie pretended my mom was making up the whole thing and said she probably did it to herself, just to cause problems. I was so ashamed of what I did. As her own daughter, I couldn't bear to hurt my mom with a true confession of the betrayal.

Although I was under an evil influence, I was still held accountable for my actions. I prayed and asked God for forgiveness for this terrible thing. I'm extremely thankful we have a God who is forgiving and true to his word. "But if we confess our sins to him, he is faithful and just to forgive us our sins and to cleanse us from all wickedness." (1 John 1:9)

Time Served

When Marc was finally released from jail six months later, he came to live in the white house with us. He knew things weren't right in that house. He witnessed the abuse and mistreatment of us all at the hands of Natalie. But his heartless, cowardly self sat quiet and did nothing to help us. In fact, he was fearful of his sister and her threats to call the police. Natalie threatened to make up lies and call the police, just to have him arrested and taken away again. She was manipulative and vindictive. Consequently, he surrendered to her demands by working for her and doing what she wanted.

Marc maintained their house, worked on their cars and assisted with money. Marc accepted a job as a semi-truck driver so he could save money to get himself, my mom, and my brother back out of the white house. He was gone for days at a time, and during those times my mom was confined to her room like a prisoner. Natalie wouldn't let her out except to get food and use the bathroom. My mom didn't have a job then, and she still didn't drive. She ate in her bedroom, slept, and watched TV. On occasion she left the house for routine doctor appointments riding the city bus for transportation.

This living arrangement lasted a couple months until my mom again left me alone at the white house. My mom moved out with Marc and my brother leaving the state of New Mexico and moving to Texas without me. They lived there for almost a year before coming back to New Mexico, and during that time, I didn't see them.

After they returned to New Mexico, I saw them about once a month. Either they came for a visit, or I went to see them. They never moved back into the white house again. I was left alone to survive my fate, living with strangers.

My heart breaks for what my mom went through all those years. She was meant to be a better mother, made for so much more. Something held her back from pursuing her goals, dreams, and desires. She lived going through the motions, barely surviving. She had no passion or energy, and I never saw her enjoy life's moments. It was like she was dead inside. I don't know what happened to her. This wasn't always who she was. I saw photos of her as a teenager and photos of her pregnant with me and after. She walked and talked with purpose, a smile on her face, and joy. But something happened to her heart and mind when she left New York. Something changed her from the inside out, and it almost killed her. She has told me her biggest regret in life was leaving New York with Marc. It was this one choice that changed her destiny and landed her on a lonely road. Because of my mom, I promised myself to be a better mother than she was. She helped me to recognize someone and something I never wanted to become: anything like her.

The End of Him

Marc made some extremely bad choices in his life, without ever showing any remorse. He never made any changes within himself to become a better person. He was cruel and devious with a criminal mind. He continued using drugs and eventually, involved in gangs. My brother witnessed him cutting off someone's fingers and torturing people. Marc spent more time in and out of jail. He continued to hurt my mom. But she lived with him; fearful for her life should she try to leave. She believed him at his word that he would find her and kill her if she ever left him.

My mom lived this way for many years, until death seemed a relief from the life she came to despise. She ultimately came to the end of herself and realized she had nothing she cared to live for. She decided she wanted to be free and have a better life. She was wiped out, worn out, exhausted physically and emotionally from being beaten, defeated and living under the hand of Marc. When she decided death was worth the risk for freedom, she left Marc after finding another man to take care of her. This man, named Tom, promised he would protect her from anyone who would try to hurt her.

Threats from Marc chased her, but no harm followed. After months of fear and intimidation, Marc finally left her alone to the new man in her life. Tom was different, but not better than Marc. He lived with his own demons in his head.

My mom lived for years as a battered woman. In fact, she stopped wearing pajamas soon after we moved to New Mexico. She went to bed in her street clothes and slept with her shoes on, changing clothes in the morning when she woke. Embarrassing as it is to tell, she still sleeps this way today. She sleeps in fear and ready to run, no matter where she is. Sadly, in battered woman's syndrome, women like my mom, have been torn down, demeaned, and controlled in abusive relationships. Some blame themselves for their abuse and pain. They don't believe they deserve anyone or anything better than the life they have. So, they seek subconsciously (and sometimes consciously) for the same characteristics in another man only to find themselves again in a similar situation of abuse.

Eventually Marc became involved in a drug cartel and vastly addicted to heroin. At the age of forty three, Marc was found dead, alone in his apartment. Heroin and drug paraphernalia were lying around the crime scene. An autopsy proved he died from a heart attack, due to an overdose of heroin. Marc's death was investigated as a possible murder case, but it was inconclusive to being accidental. The truth is, Marc died an untimely tragic death due to his wicked, depraved heart, his horrific choices, and his illicit principles.

Marc's funeral arrangements were organized in the cheapest manner possible, because there was no money for the expenses. My mom attended his funeral with resentment and bitterness but she felt obligated to say her last good-bye. I don't know what she felt while she was at his funeral. I'd like to imagine she felt relief and freedom; but emotional pain can be agonizing and keep us prisoners to our restless and anxious minds. Memories can haunt us and make past events vividly come alive. I don't know if she has forgiven Marc for all he did to her. The only freedom any of us will ever experience is when we forgive. There is freedom in forgiveness. I've forgiven Marc for all he did and didn't do for me.

12
The Babysitter

Beginning at the age of nine, I was a delegated child care provider at the white house. We provided day care for ten to fourteen children per day in an underground babysitting service. Natalie and Elizabeth didn't have a license to run a day care. They were paid under the table, exceeding the number of children allowed per state law.

The children were dropped off early in the morning, some as early as 5am and all were picked up by 6pm. The parents never knew the truth concerning how many children were there at one time. Natalie and Elizabeth lied, saying the number of children they watched was between six and eight. These parents handed over their babies and diaper bags at the door. They left their small, defenseless children into the hands of strangers. When parents came to pick up their children early, I'd have to hide in another room and not come out until they left. Because I was kept home from school often to help watch the kids, the parents couldn't find out I was there. The children's ages ranged from newborn to six years old. Elizabeth and Natalie didn't like caring for older children because they could talk and tell.

The kids spent the day playing with toys and watching TV. There was an outdoor patio where they colored, ate their snack, and played games. I sat down with the kids watching shows like, "You and Me Kid," "Dumbo's Circus," cartoons, and assorted kids' movies. Lunch often consisted of peanut butter sandwiches with apricot jelly, ramen noodle soup, grilled cheese sandwiches, or macaroni and cheese.

Nap time came in the early afternoon; all children and babies were put in one room. Some kids slept in multiple numbers on the bed, some on the floor. If the kids didn't lie down or the babies cried, Elizabeth or Natalie would go into the room with a big wooden spoon and hit them. They said to spank the kids on the diaper or butt only, and never leave a mark on the back leg. I didn't want to spank the kids; I couldn't do it, especially the helpless infants who lay in their cribs. I saw Elizabeth and Natalie beat on those poor kids.

We were all helpless kids; I was just one of them. When the parents came at pick up time, I wanted so badly to warn them to get their children out of there. I wanted them to know how their babies were treated. Those poor children were unable to defend themselves or even speak for themselves. It is beyond understanding, why they too, had to live under the wrath and influence of the white house wickedness.

Accidents happen, and this particular incident haunts my memories. During lunch time Elizabeth was in the kitchen and had a large kettle of boiling water on the stove with ramen noodles. I was outside the glass sliding doors on the back patio play area with most of the kids. We were picking up toys and getting ready for lunch when I heard horrific screams piercing my ears and giving me chills. I ran into the kitchen. One of the toddlers had reached up and pulled the boiling pot of soup on top of her. Her small, delicate Hawaiian arm was severely burned; skin was peeled back and hanging from her arm. Her whole arm was intensely burned and she was writhing in pain. Elizabeth put a cold cloth on her arm, picked her up and they rushed her to the emergency room while leaving me alone with the rest of the kids. Natalie and Elizabeth were petrified of what her parents would do. I don't know what ever happened to the little girl because she never came back to our day-care.

That illegal day care is one of the reasons I attended so many different grade schools. I was often kept home from school to help care for the children. Elizabeth and Natalie used me to feed babies, change diapers, play games with the kids, make bottles, pick up toys, clean up, wipe green snotty noses, watch TV with them, and even dispense prescribed medications. Sometimes I was left alone with the kids while they went out to run errands or to a doctor's appointment. When the school started calling and asking why I wasn't in attendance, Elizabeth and Natalie sent me back for awhile, then transferred me to another local school, providing a fake home address. Natalie drove me to school, or I took a school bus. When the school was far away, I rode a city bus alone.

Monsters under the Bed

The strangers left me home alone sometimes. Being left home alone can cause boredom, and boredom can breed foolish actions. Because it was off limits, I was curious to know what was in Natalie's bedroom; she was secretive about her territory. While snooping around, I looked under her bed and found monsters in the form of pornographic magazines. Magazines littered with naked women!

Out of curiosity, I looked at the magazines and it tainted my view of sexuality. It created in my mind a perversion of sex instead of the beauty God intended to be between a married man and woman. It is beyond doubt and argument pornography destroys our minds and hearts. It was destroying mine. I didn't view those magazines once or twice, but often. It became something exciting for me to do when I had time alone in the house. Pornography was a temptation which lured me back over and over again and ate away at my mind and soul. I knew it had to be wrong because of the way it made me feel, hence one of the reasons it was hidden. While wrong and secretive, it enticed me; it fed my curiosity and even set me up for experimentation with boys and some girls at an earlier age than expected by "normal" society. This was all before my twelfth birthday. Being young I didn't happen to question the gender of the pornography. It was a long time after, I was able to put some pieces to the puzzle together and come to the conclusion: Natalie was a lesbian.

Looking back at how viewing pornography made me feel, in one word, the experience made me feel "less." I felt worthless and useless. It reduced whatever self-esteem I had to zero. At first, visually it modeled something that appeared thrilling and enticing, however realistically it was unachievable. I remember lusting not after the sex but after wanting to look like the women I saw. I felt like a war raged inside me, I wanted to look just like those women, but looking at my body in the mirror brought the disappointment of thinking it would never happen.

There was a lure of curiosity to sexual parts of the pornography; they seemed exciting, new, and different. I had never seen anything like this, but sadly it only created a hunger of lust so deep it was impossible to fulfill. The more I fed it, the more I wanted it; the more I felt empty, the less I felt satisfied. Instead, I felt dirty, corrupt, and guilty. Not knowing it at the time, the "Holy Spirit" was watching over me. He revealed my feelings and helped me realize how wrong it was and enabled me to stop looking at pornography. I eventually felt so wrong and guilty for looking at it, and I didn't want to feel that way anymore.

The need to be more than I am was not just created by pornography. I had a void needing to be filled. Many women suffer from this hunger. I've often wondered over the years where this need – to be "more than whom God created" – came from. I've contemplated why I couldn't be happy or content with how God made me. The more I sought the world and its view of "beauty," the more I felt less and was disappointed. It began with Eve in the Garden of Eden when she was tempted by Satan. I realize I'm now under a curse as all women are because of this great fall taken by Eve. While enduring deception and temptation, Eve began to question her personal knowledge. She wasn't content with knowing only good; she felt insecure being left out from what God was holding back. Aren't we all like this at times? I certainly was when I entered that bedroom and sought out something hidden. I was curious to know what was secret, what was concealed. I look back and now wish my eyes were veiled from such images.

When we yield to temptation there is always a consequence. Mine have been years of fighting feelings of inner despair and rejection. I became tainted all the more because of the sinful presence in my life and my own curiosity to know helped bring me down. A child's surroundings matter to their spiritual choices in life. I was surrounded by evil and evil made its impact on my heart and soul. Yet, I am forever thankful God was in my midst. "My help comes from the Lord, who made heaven and earth!" (Psalm 121:2)

Stripped of all my Beauty

Head lice are extremely contagious and unfortunately I caught it from the day care children at the white house. I had beautiful, long, wavy blonde hair just like my mother's. When Natalie found the lice she decided my hair was too long and too much work for her to treat. She sat me on the toilet seat in the bathroom and chopped off my hair with scissors. She combed it out, yanked it, and pulled it. It certainly wasn't pleasant or done in a caring manner. She didn't care about me or my hair full of bugs. I was treated like I was being punished for catching lice. I sat in shock watching parts of me fall to the ground. My hair was turned into a pixie cut, and now I looked like a boy. I was humiliated and embarrassed to walk outside the house. Most days I wore a knit hat to hide my disgraceful head.

I lived in a body, but it wasn't my own. Natalie had taken control over me and did whatever she wanted. No one stopped her, not even her own mother. On a warm, summer day, I had my bathing suit on, getting ready to enjoy a swim. Natalie got angry for some reason and started beating on me. I happened to get my hands in her way and accidently scratched her arm. She was extremely angry because I caused a mark on her. She grabbed me and took me into the bathroom while she yelled, "You will no longer have long nails!" Natalie pulled the nail clippers from the medicine cabinet. One by one cut off my pretty, long nails. I sat with tears streaming down my face as I watched. My nails were a small part of beauty upon my body I admired. She stripped me of the only thing making me feel beautiful.

Losing my hair and nails made me feel ugly and unwanted. I found myself hoping no one would look at me. I hid myself from people because I was embarrassed and ashamed. Without my long, pretty hair, I felt disfigured like a part of my identity was stolen. My self-esteem was low. When I looked into the mirror, I cried and harbored resentment towards myself because of my weakness. I wanted desperately to control the situations and fight Natalie back, but I couldn't. I wanted to make the abuse stop, but nothing within me was strong enough. As a child I was unable to comprehend that I was simply not equipped to fight back.

Now, I realize I began to develop unachievable and unrealistic expectations of myself throughout childhood. This led me into perfectionism and being an over-achiever. I used perfectionism to protect myself in hopes of never again becoming a failure, being criticized, weak or being disapproved.

Sweat Dreams

Summer nights were hot and muggy. Perspiration dripped from my forehead as I rested on my pillow. Most nights I was privileged to sleep with the relief of a box fan blowing on my face. This comforting breeze on my sunburned face and the gentle humming from the fan helped my anxious mind to rest. Many times after I'd drift off to sleep I was suddenly awakened by Natalie. She would beat me up in my bed, pull my hair, slap me around, scratch, or hurt me in cruel ways. That experience was like some kind of malicious shock treatment I had to endure without sedation. I was tormented for years with demonic nightmares. I often dreamed of being chased by the devil, and when I woke up I saw him outside my window looking at me. That part was real. He was hunting me, watching me, and instilling an intense fear into my being keeping me from peace and sleep.

From a young age, I lived in constant fear. My sleep was affected dramatically because of my abuse. I was afraid to close my eyes at night because I feared I would die while I slept. The only way I could fall asleep was repeating over and over, "Jesus loves me. Jesus loves me." I'd say "Jesus loves me" hundreds of times until my exhausted mind would give in and drift off to sleep.

The bedroom where I slept was cluttered and dirty; the aura of the room had a distinct evil and unsettling feeling. I know demons resided in that house. The dark and frightening demons in my dreams were the same ones I saw in the bedroom when I'd wake up in the night screaming. They hovered above me and appeared as clouds of darkness. I'd scream and tremor in my bed until they went away. They never touched or physically harmed me but I have no doubt they persuaded Natalie to act on their behalf.

Safe in His Arms

The constant phrase "Jesus Loves Me" kept me safe in God's arms. I see now the power of His name gave me comfort and help. During countless nights I was visited and tormented by real evil and its presence. God held me in His arms and protected me from eternal harm. Even though I experienced what I did, I know worse could've happened. I lived in the reality of God's word. "We are pressed on every side by troubles, but we are not crushed. We are perplexed, but not driven to despair. We are hunted down, but never abandoned by God. We get knocked down, but we are not destroyed." (2 Corinthians 4:8-9)

Desperate Measures

Day after day I lived in continuous torture, physical pain, and emotional agony. As a child of only eleven years old, I had no escape. I made plans in my mind to find a way to safety, but no matter how hard I worked at trying to find a solution, nothing seemed to make sense. One option did make sense: remove the harm itself. In that case I'd need to remove Natalie from the equation. I hated her with a passion. I had a will to survive and a heart wanting to be free. I knew the life I was living wasn't normal or good. I felt exhausted and always unsettled, waiting for the next bad thing to happen.

Finally, I thought I was going to get a break from my pain. Natalie became sick and endured days of abdominal pain, nausea, and vomiting. She became sick enough to need a doctor immediately, so we took her to the emergency room. I was in the room with her when a nurse was taking her vital signs and asking her medical questions. Natalie told the nurse she was allergic to penicillin, and if she took this medication, she would get sick or die. My first thought was, "I hope they give her some." Natalie had surgery to remove her gallbladder. She got well and returned home after a few days and bragged about her new abdominal scar. She was proud of her large incision with the staples and enjoyed the attention of showing it off.

Not long after Natalie's surgery, Elizabeth went to the dentist with severe tooth pain. She found out she had an abscessed tooth, and the dentist placed her on penicillin to treat the infection. Elizabeth put the penicillin in the kitchen cabinet where all the medications were kept. My thoughts ran wild with ideas about how I could get Natalie to take some penicillin if she hurt me ever again.

Natalie left red marks, bruises, scratches, and evidence on my body I despised. It would only remind me of the reality of my pain. This time was the last time I'd ever allow Natalie to hurt me again. I declared and made a promise to myself that I wouldn't let her harm me anymore. In the middle of the night I snuck out of bed while everyone was sleeping. I stole some penicillin pills from Elizabeth's bottle, crushed them up and put them in a two liter bottle of Natalie's coke. In the morning I waited in awkward anticipation for her to go to the fridge for a drink as on any day with her normal routine.

Natalie grabbed the bottle and poured some in a glass. She took one sip and complained the soda was flat and dumped the remainder of the bottle in the sink. Fortunately for Natalie, my plan failed, and she escaped her demise. This was a desperate attempt to save my own life from the slow death I was living every day. I never thought of the consequences or understood my own thinking. I just wanted to be safe somehow.

As I sit with tears in my eyes, I pray for my heart to be healed and also yours! If you have a painful past, be brave with me and surrender it all to Jesus. Trust him and be expectant for healing and great things to come!

Moment of Truth

One of the hardest things in life we have to face can be our past. What happens when we get alone with ourselves, our past, and our feelings? For me this can be an emotionally draining and painful time. It's hard to mentally go back to the times we wish never happened. If only we could shake the pain or erase some memories. But if we let our past control us, it can defeat us. We can't make it go away, but we can let God heal and restore our hearts. God can make us whole! He can give us peace that surpasses all understanding and joy unspeakable. "Don't worry about anything; instead, pray about everything. Tell God what you need, and thank him for all he has done." (Philippians 4:6-7)

13

Food for Thought

Food was a main focus in my childhood. Our lives were centered on it because we lived in a feast or famine reality. We frequented restaurants with buffets when we dined out. At the buffets we were encouraged to eat as much as possible to get our money's worth. Our stomachs weren't the only things we filled up; we stole food from the buffets and put it in large purses or bags. We carried the food back home to provide meals for the next few days.

In the kitchen of the white house was a special, forbidden table of snacks off limits to all of us kids. It was a large, brown, dull finished round kitchen table full of junk food. It was a tempting sight full of life's simple pleasures which would satisfy not only the taste buds, but also temporarily numb any negative emotions. Chocolate, candy, cake, pies, and treats of all kinds filled the table. The table was off limits to us kids. To avoid the heartache of denial, I stole snacks frequently to fulfill my desires. I loved to sneak things off the table and eat them in secret. When I ate from the table wonderful sensations would rush over me. I felt my heart beat fast and my hands tremble with excitement. I enjoyed a rush of happiness for a short moment. My mind was temporarily released from my fear, worries, and pain. I looked forward to this every day and the brief escape from the oppressive reality I lived.

Over time I became a chunky child. I wasn't obese, but I carried some extra pounds. I had no healthy choices or positive influences to assist me in proper health and wellness. I was forced to eat whatever was on my plate. This became a problem interfering with my ability to recognize hunger and fullness signals. These kinds of bad habits set me up early for unhealthy eating, weight gain, and eating disorders. Abnormal and unhealthy eating became one of my biggest struggles and trials overwhelming my life for years.

Having to overcome these obstacles in life has made me an advocate for education in health and wellness. It's important for us to know how to properly care for our bodies with appropriate nutrition and exercise. It's also essential for any of us with children to teach our kids healthy eating habits. We greatly influence our children and they will model our behavior. We can't eat a box of cookies and then suggest to our kids to eat an apple. It isn't right for us to spend five hours on the couch watching TV and then yell at our kids for spending five hours playing video games. It may sound unfair and not what you want to hear, but kids don't want someone to just tell them what to do. They want a role model.

Part of being a parent is teaching. As a matter of fact, every one of us is a teacher whether we think so or not. Somebody learns something from each of us. If you are a parent or influence anyone, what are you teaching? When it comes to health and wellness, it's helpful if we teach what to do, how to do it, and why. Explain how to choose proper foods and the benefits of healthy snacks. Don't think just because someone doesn't seem to be responding to you, they are not listening. We teach others by our actions and not just by our words.

14
Enough is Enough

*W*hen I was thirteen years old I had enough. I could no longer live in my abusive life tolerating the way I was treated. I couldn't take it anymore. I spent days, weeks, and months thinking and trying to figure out how to get out of my abusive situation. I searched the yellow pages for airlines and wanted to call and find out prices of tickets. I tried to figure out how to get money and where I could go with a plane ticket, if I could get one. There was no way at my age I could maneuver a plan of escape or even maintain an independent living situation. I'd have ended up on the streets, a prostitute, or homeless. I couldn't think logically. I desperately yearned to be free and my thinking ran wild with crazy ideas.

On a Saturday evening at the white house my brother was visiting. Natalie packed up a box of items for us to go door-to-door and sell. As Natalie's "little servants," my brother and I put on our shoes and set out to make her some money. We crossed a main street a couple blocks away and this led us to some nice homes in a subdivision. We talked about Natalie, and James told me she had beaten him up recently, and many times before. I was angry and sad for my brother's pain, I wanted to save him but I didn't know how. I hadn't realized what he'd been enduring too. I wanted to protect my little brother and stand up for myself. I vowed we would never go back to the white house again, Natalie wouldn't hurt us anymore. I didn't have a game plan, only the ambition to run away. I was adamant and meant exactly what I said. I told James we were never going back.

While walking around the subdivision we came upon a friend's home. We stopped to talk, and he invited us in. His older teenage brother came down the stairs to greet us. Their parents weren't home, so we stayed to hang out. My little brother eventually became discontent warning that we better leave to get back home or we'd be in trouble. I had immense determination within me at that point; I didn't even fear the thought of Natalie anymore. I was angry and tired. I wasn't going to let her hurt me or control my life any longer. I made my brother stay with me longer, fearlessly hanging out. More boys kept coming over, and we found out the boys living there were alone for the weekend with a party planned.

The Perfect Storm

Hours passed, and it soon became the dark of night. We played games, talked, ate food and ran around outside playing flashlight tag. What an amazing breath of fresh air (literally), and an experience of freedom.

That night around ten o'clock, we were outside and saw a helicopter flying low with a spot light shinning from it, sweeping our surrounding area. Something deep inside my gut told me it was looking for us. I took my brother inside the house and never mentioned the possibility of the helicopter searching for us. I didn't want to freak out my brother. I was scared but not convinced to go back home. I asked the oldest brother who was sixteen, for permission to stay and sleep over that night.

I definitely wasn't using logic or any common sense when I put myself in that situation. I was permitted to sleep in one of the boy's bedrooms, and he would sleep downstairs. Later that night, three older boys came into the bedroom and started talking sweetly and touching me. They asked and pleaded with me to have sex with them and assured me they wouldn't get me pregnant. I said no. Feeling disgusted, I refused to have sex with them. They persisted, especially the oldest one who was sixteen and pushed himself on top of me and laid there. All three boys took turns kissing and molesting me. I wasn't strong enough to force them off and no adult was home to help or hear me yell. I didn't scream out, I just laid there quietly and helplessly waiting for everything to end. I felt shame and guilt. And for a long time, I felt responsible for what happened. I blamed myself and believed it was my fault because I chose to stay at that house.

During therapy years ago, I finally forgave myself and now understand it wasn't my fault. I never asked, wanted, or planned to be assaulted. If a girl goes to a bar and gets raped in the bathroom, is it her fault she was raped? No. It is not. She may have placed herself in a dangerous or promiscuous situation, but she was a victim and she was violated.

The next morning when we woke up, my brother and I were on the local news. We were missing and presumed kidnapped. Our mother was on T.V. in front of a microphone, holding our photos and pleading for her children back. I felt no remorse for her. If she was so upset and sad we were gone, then why didn't she take better care of us before? I didn't like my mother. I rather despised her and had no guilt for making her cry. It was her turn to cry and hurt like I had for all those years. Natalie was standing next to my mom in front of the news camera. I had hatred so great for that woman for all she had done to me and my brother. She was psychotic and a fake appearing to support my mother. I knew who she really was.

The boys saw the news and were in shock about the whole situation. They didn't realize what they got themselves into. They wanted no part of trouble and told us we had to leave, especially before their parents got home.

Desperately, I began searching for an immediate solution. "Where would we go and what should we do?" After thinking, I was inspired by my own creativity based on how I was taught to solve problems: my idea included lying and manipulation.

Mentally, I planned out our next steps. It began raining which assisted in making our story more believable. I ripped holes in my pants and shirt and tore my brother's clothes too. I hit myself creating bruises on my body, stomped in mud puddles to get dirty, and made myself fall causing my knee to bleed. We left the house and ventured out about a mile away to a convenience store called Circle K. When we arrived at Circle K, missing person flyers of us were taped on the store door. (That's a picture of yourself you never want to see.) I walked up to the store clerk crying and asked them to call the police. I pointed out we were the kids on the flyer and needed help. They called the police and stood by us as we waited for them to arrive. The police took us into their care and drove us to the police station where they questioned us and called our mom. I made up a story with my brother before we turned ourselves in that we were prepared to tell. At the police station they separated my brother and me. I was totally unaware they separated us for the purpose of individual questioning to investigate what happened while we were missing.

We told the police while we were on a walk; we were kidnapped by three men in a white van. The men pulled over and forced us into the van. Then they drove us out to the middle of the desert near a water park. The men made us sleep alone in the van at night, and beat us up the next morning after realizing they didn't need to keep us any longer. They drove us a couple miles away and dumped us out of the van. We ran fast to the nearest store and called the police.

The police didn't believe our story. Our stories didn't match each other's, and my brother broke down. They locked him in a cell and demanded he tell the truth or they told him he would have to stay there. My little brother told the whole truth. We were released into my mom's custody, and she and Marc drove us back to their apartment.

Even though we told the police about being abused, they didn't help us. Maybe my mom convinced them we were lying to protect herself. After spending a couple days with my mom, I overheard her on the payphone talking. Apparently after I told the police why I ran away and about all the abuse, Elizabeth and Natalie refused me back to their home. My mom didn't want me either and decided it was best if she contacted my dad to ask if he would take me into his care.

My mom made a desperate phone call to my dad who lived in the state of New York. To my dismay after eight years, she not only knew where he lived, but she had his phone number! What an unbelievable mess, such betrayal and deceit from my own mother. I don't know exactly what story my mom told my dad. But I do know she asked him to consider taking me into his care. He said he needed time to speak with his new wife, but he was sure he wanted his daughter back. He requested my brother come, too, but my mom refused. My brother and my mom were close; there was no way she would send him off with me. Just one day later, it was decided I'd go live with my father and start a new life.

Freedom in Forgiveness

Freedom to me means being out from under control of people. I desire to live a life of freedom: free to be, free to do, free to speak, free to act, and free to think on my own and for myself.

I was in bondage as a prisoner for a long time. I was taken advantage of, used, abused, mistreated, and controlled by others. After I was finally set free from the physical bondage, I was unfortunately still a prisoner to the emotional and mental pain, torment and memories. I needed help and healing. I had many things in my mind to work through, things to let go of and people to forgive. My pain and issues required counseling which helped me tremendously.

Never be ashamed or too embarrassed to get counseling. When you get the help you need you are being strong and wise. If you believe you need help, don't hesitate to seek it out. You are your own best advocate. You may have to try more than one person who fits your personality, issues, or beliefs. But don't give up. There is someone out there God has ready and willing to help you. Pray, get references, and be your own advocate! You are worth it!!

Living in freedom may require us to make hard choices. One of the hardest choices I've made in life is forgiving Natalie. I'm exceptionally glad I forgave Natalie for all she did to me before she died on February 14, 2012.

Curiosity got the best of me while I was writing this book. I decided to do a web search on Natalie hoping to find a picture or information. I was looking for something to help me gain more understanding or add pieces to the puzzle in my mind about her. Shockingly, what I came across was her obituary and a lonely online guest book with only six people's condolences.

Seeing her obituary made me feel like I was in a black hole, a place of total nothingness. At first, I felt nothing. I literally looked at the computer with a blank stare, my mind empty and my mouth open without words to speak. It took me a few minutes to grasp the reality of the news. Then I felt the shock. I couldn't believe she was dead. I wondered how she died. Where? What time? Was anyone with her? Death in her family once again came at an early age. Death took

Natalie at age fifty-three. I can't see her, talk to her, call her, visit, or ever look into her eyes again to say anything. It's not that I ever planned on doing any of that, but now I couldn't, even if I wanted to.

It's still hard to accept she's dead. Maybe it's because she still lives vivid in my mind, and memories of her torment me. I'm not smiling or happy about her death. I had thought in the past that once she died I'd have a sense of relief and peace, and I'd finally feel safe from her. The truth is her death only makes me sad. I know she was miserable inside and she had a horrible life. I found out from a reliable source she had been living with another woman before she died, and they may have been lovers.

Even though I'm unaware of the condition of her heart upon her death, I'm prepared on the day I arrive in heaven to spend eternity with Natalie should she be there. God allows me to feel empathy and compassion for her brokenness and the pain she carried deep in her heart. I forgive her for what she did to me. Something was severely wrong with her. Maybe she had been abused herself and had never known love. But I experienced her wrath, and I felt her pain. I witnessed and experienced an evil and desolate entity enticing her thoughts and actions. I could hate her and be angry and bitter. I could despise her and want her to burn in Hell forever. But what good would that do? The desire for vengeance will do nothing except keep me in bondage to emotional turmoil and unforgiveness. The Bible is clear about forgiveness. "If you forgive those who sin against you, your heavenly Father will forgive you." (Matthew 6:14)

I've learned forgiveness is a choice and not a feeling. I take Natalie to the cross of Jesus and leave her at His feet. At the cross I also leave my pain, sorrow, and my own brokenness. I hand over my despair, questions and hurting soul. I ask and trust God to heal me, restore me, prosper me, love me, and make me whole. I'm not saying all this to make myself look good. And I'm not lying to myself. I know what it's like to carry around bitterness and unforgiveness. It's heavy, burdensome, dark, and sinful. I choose to forgive as Christ has forgiven me for all my sins.

I don't know where Natalie is today. Heaven or Hell has her. What I do know for sure is where I am today. I'm walking in freedom, love, power and peace that exceeds all understanding!

I am free.

15
My New Family

My dad bought me a one-way plane ticket from New Mexico to upstate New York. I boarded the plane alone without luggage, wearing only the clothes on my back and a pair of beat up purple jelly shoes on my feet. I was in good health except my distraught emotional state and a badly infected toe needing medical attention. I tearfully waved goodbye to my mom and brother while getting on the plane. I was unaware it was the last time for the next seven years I'd have any contact with them.

The plane ride was lonely, frightening, and long. I was anxious and all alone for my first flight. I knew nothing about my new family or even what my dad looked like. I tried my best to be brave and optimistically consider my new life with my dad, stepmom, and step brothers.

The landing gear went down and the plane hit the ground for a bumpy, but safe landing. I walked off the plane alone, confused, and scared. No one was running up to hug me or greet me as I saw others being greeted. I wandered around for awhile close to the gate noticing how cold the air felt against my face.

A few minutes passed, but it felt like an hour. I glanced across the terminal and saw a somewhat familiar face looking at my own. I stood still while a man started to slowly walk toward me and call out, "Brooke?" I nodded my head and said, "Yes." The man walked up to me, grabbed a hold of me in a meaningful way, and gave me a big hug, but it felt awkward. Behind him followed his wife and her two sons.

We drove two hours from the airport through wind and snow to get to their house. During that time, we all talked about ourselves to become acquainted. I was in awe of my new family and how "normal" their lives appeared to be compared to the way I was used to living. My dad and stepmom had careers, owned a home and vehicles. The boys regularly attended the same school, played sports, and also had gaming equipment I'd only seen in stores. This kind of living sounded like a great opportunity. I smiled inside and imagined I'd finally have all I'd ever wanted and dreamed: a real loving, normal family, free from pain.

When we arrived at their home, I was in awe of the new reality I entered. We drove into a glamorous subdivision with many nice houses. The inside of their home was large, spotless, organized, had all the utilities on, and food filled the cupboards and refrigerator. My dad encouraged me to call the house my own home, and I was allowed to eat and drink whatever and whenever I wanted. I felt like "Annie" who had just moved in with "Daddy Warbucks. "

A Different Way

It was an enormous change to encounter organization, structure, a secure family, and also a new climate. Since I had no clothes, my dad and stepmom took me shopping to the mall for new ones. They bought me fashionable, neat, and clean clothing. The clothes made me feel good about myself, and I was thankful to look so nice.

The time of my move occurred during the eighth grade. The new school I would attend required me to take placement tests. This would reveal what grade level I was functioning on since I had previously missed so much school. The tests concluded I was behind in my education, and the school district required me to spend the whole upcoming summer in summer school catching up. It was essentially worth the time and energy to be placed in the right grade and not held behind. I was grateful for the opportunity.

In my new house I had my own bedroom with furniture, a TV, and even a phone. I had new clothes, jewelry, shoes, and beauty essentials. I went from poverty to riches in material possessions. However, even though I had all that stuff, I still felt empty and lonely inside. I craved and desired relationships with people, and I wanted to belong to a family who cared about me and not just provided things. I learned quickly the things of this world are not what truly satisfies or gives us joy and fulfillment. I was deeply disheartened to not be loved and adored as I had always longed to be. Time made it apparent my dad and stepmom didn't know how to place more value and importance in people and relationships than material possessions.

Contentment

This brings us to an, "Ah, ha!" moment when we can ask God to examine our hearts and ask ourselves, "Can I ever be content?" Spoiler alert: The answer is yes!

The world we live in is competitive, jealous, and discontent. People constantly compare themselves with others and measure their social importance in regards to who has the most and biggest material assets. Society has created unrealistic goals and expectations designed to meet man's requirements for daily happiness.

There is undoubtedly a time when we have wanted something newer, bigger, or better just to have it. We have also wanted things just because we see someone else with them. As we look out our house windows and see the neighbors upgrade, we immediately become jealous and wonder how they afford or even deserve what they have. The newest make and model vehicles drive up and down the streets as we drool over them with envy. Delivery trucks roar by after dropping off the latest online shopping packages. We compete with neighbors and insist on having the best lawn in the subdivision no matter the water bill cost. The younger generations are adamantly "gung ho" on owning the latest phone, iPad, iPod, purse, shoes, or trendy item. We don't readily and outright admit jealousy, lust, or greed, but it's a real internal battle we fight.

We need to stop trying to "keep up with the Joneses" and learn to receive contentment and fulfillment from Jesus. He alone knows what we need. "And this same God who takes care of you will supply all your needs from his glorious riches, which have been given to you in Christ Jesus." (Philippians 4:19) We shouldn't strive, struggle, and go into debt to have things we don't need and can't afford. It's unnecessary to try to impress or prove ourselves to people by the possessions we own or even by the brand of clothes we wear.

If you desire more joy and a better outlook on life; learn to live as God instructs. "Don't store up treasures here on earth, where moths eat them and rust destroys them and where thieves break in and steal. But store your treasures in heaven, where moths and rust cannot destroy, and thieves do not break in and steal." (Matthew 6:19) Eternal treasures include loving, being compassionate, courageously inviting someone to church, helping to meet people's needs, pouring into relationships, spending time with family and friends, and simply living out what Jesus says: "'And you must love the Lord your God with all your heart, all your soul, all your mind, and all your strength.' The second is equally important: 'Love your neighbor as yourself.' No other commandment is greater than these." (Mark 12:30-31)

Material possessions in themselves are not a sin. What matters is what we make of them. Putting anything above God has a potential to become an idol. Contentment and knowing who you are in Christ is the key to living happily with what you have rather than being dissatisfied and seeking to be fulfilled by things or people. "Seek the Kingdom of God above all else, and live righteously, and he will give you everything you need." (Matthew 6:33)

16
Family Matters

My dad took pride in himself, what he owned and his personal accomplishments. He didn't put our family first and wasn't true to his word. When he promised to be home for dinner or attend an event, you couldn't count on him. My dad spent long hours hunting and too much time with his buddies.

My dad spoke ugly and rudely about people with judgment; he never saw himself as wrong and wouldn't accept anyone else's opinion. He thought he had all the answers, and no one was allowed to question him. Profanity came loosely from his lips. He didn't care what he said to anyone or how it affected them. He intentionally chose to hurt me by speaking disrespectful and hurtful things about my mother. He selfishly tormented me with his relentless words and anger towards my mom coming from his own indwelling pain. He blamed my mom for all their previous problems and refused to accept any responsibility for their failed marriage. He was certainly not the mentor in my life I needed or expected him to be.

Smack Down

My step brothers and I had some fun times but also the common brother-sister rivalries. One evening we were arguing and our yelling carried on longer than my dad could tolerate listening to from another room. My dad came into the room yelling at us, and I responded with sarcasm. He came at me strong and hit me across the room. He told me it was his house; he pointed his finger in my face and furiously said, "I will knock your teeth out."

My dad took that moment as an opportunity to put his foot down and demand respect from a daughter he didn't know. He tried to obtain immediate control to prevent any future circumstances that may arise between us, where he would be, or could be, undermined. With his rage and uncontrolled behavior, he didn't earn my respect or show me the discipline I needed. I already knew what it was like to be beaten up, what I needed was a safe home with unconditional love.

Janet was my stepmom. She had a small frame, curly hair, and it was colored sandy blonde from a do-it-yourself box. Her body resembled one of a retired ballet dancer. She was a woman of few words, stern in her behavior, and walked around with a chip on her shoulder. I could sense by the way she treated me and looked into my eyes I wasn't the daughter she always dreamed of having. It was all too obvious I was quite an invasion in her life and not what she planned for when she married my dad five years earlier.

From the beginning, Janet spoke indecent words about me. Our bedrooms were next door and I eavesdropped on my new parents conversations. Janet often questioned my dad's reasoning for bringing me into their home. She was fearful to find out what kind of child I was and the troubles I carried from my broken past. It became clear that instead of being happy for my dad or me, Janet was fearful and unsettled by my presence.

Janet's attitude towards me grew more harsh and cold; I received glaring looks and short answers for communication. My first impressions of a cozy environment quickly faded into an uneasy atmosphere of feeling unwanted and insecure. I performed my best always trying to do well, winning Janet's love and approval. I worked hard at the chores I was given, kept the house especially clean, and tried to keep my mouth shut around her because nothing I spoke was appreciated.

Around Janet I had to pretend to be quiet and reserved, but in reality I was outgoing, talkative, and energetic. I wasn't able to be myself. In Janet's presence, I was scared to do or say the next thing wrong and get in trouble. I was simply unacceptable to her liking.

Around the Clock

During the weekdays Karl and Janet held full time jobs while my step brothers and I attended school. Making friends was hard due to being the new girl. I felt vulnerable and the need to be guarded. I had learned to keep people at a distance and trusted no one completely.

My weekends consisted of cleaning, spending time with a couple neighborhood girls, and babysitting. Sunday's were just part of the weekend for us and not a family worship day. My new family didn't go to church or even talk about God and there wasn't a "Joy Bus" to pick me up.

Thankfully, even though I didn't go to church, I knew God. I prayed and on occasion I read the Bible. In my heart I knew there was more to life than what the world offered. In my heart was a longing and a desire to become closer to God and know him more.

During my childhood, the world disappointed me and proved to be unstable and cruel with little to offer. I was troubled with the disappointment I continued to experience. I was a lost and hurting child inside waiting for my daddy to pick me up, hug me and love me. I had convinced myself and believed my dad was going to be the best thing that ever happened to me. I put my hope, trust, and expectations in a man to love and protect me. I moved from New Mexico, leaving behind nothing, in anticipation of gaining everything. I was broken, and I thought a dad would help make me whole. I thought owning the name "father" or "dad" would motivate him to live with higher standards and a commitment to love. Being a dad carried with it certain responsibilities and duties to be fulfilled. I opened my heart to this man in weakness, desperation, and pain. But instead of him helping my heart to heal, he broke it even more. I had nothing to offer, and sadly that is exactly what I got back from the one who was supposed to teach me about love, life, and family.

One may consider I'm being insensitive and tearing apart the man who bought me a one-way airline ticket and vowed to take in his thirteen year old daughter no one else wanted. Or maybe someone may judge me and deem me unable to perceive things in a realistic manner because of my past. I beg to differ as I venture into sharing a painful time when I was taunted, unaccepted, judged, and emotionally mistreated by my dad and stepmom.

17
Daddy's Little Girl

On most occasions a gift is a remarkable thing to receive. There are no expectations to give a gift back and the best gifts are the ones you did nothing to deserve. However, have you ever received a gift with strings attached? You may have wanted to give it back because it caused more trouble than it was worth. Maybe the person who gave you the gift threw the expense in your face all the time. Maybe they gave it with selfish intentions.

My dad wouldn't let me enjoy or gratefully accept his gift for the one-way plane ticket from New Mexico to New York. My dad was certain he was the one who single-handedly and ultimately saved my life. He constantly demanded I should thank him for the rest of my days. He bragged while telling the story about how his "little girl" got off the plane with rags for clothes, old jelly shoes, and an infected toe. He believed he rescued me from the pit of Hell. He said I was nothing, and I had nothing without him. He made sure to always remind me of his heroic act.

Please be assured I told him "thank you" plenty of times, and I meant it. But I became mentally exhausted from listening to him glorify himself and gloat of his good works. He did help me, and I don't know where I'd be today without his intervention. I'm forever grateful for his act of kindness. If only the guilt he put on me after giving me the gift wasn't so difficult to carry around.

Spotless

My stepmom had a fetish with cleaning; her home had to be spotless all the time. The floors were her main focus. She walked around picking up small pieces of string, paper, dirt, and even the tiniest particles. Saturday mornings, and numerous times in between, Janet would clean the house, do the laundry, empty the cat litter box, wash the dishes, and more. This wasn't just every day housework; it was unwarranted cleaning done under the influence of perfectionism. I watched in confusion at first, but after some time I recognized the satisfaction and appreciation Janet established with cleaning and its outcome. I desired to gain Janet's approval, so perfectionism became my standard, too.

Eventually all the housework became my responsibility. It was an excessive amount of work expected to be done by one teenager. It was unclear why the duties weren't shared among all of us kids, but I didn't dispute things I was told to do. After all, where would I have been without my new family? Cleaning made me feel satisfied and accomplished. I felt like I had to work as hard as possible so I could earn my stay and contribute my fair share in the home.

The expectations placed on me kept me from being a teenager and enjoying life. I was treated differently from my step brothers. I wasn't included in fun events like they were. My consequences were more demanding than theirs. I was grounded and unable to make plans if things weren't done exactly as Janet required. Her standards were unreachable. She was a perfectionist who set high expectations for herself and everyone else, except her sons. My friends jokingly nicknamed me "Cinderella" and the name fit, just like the shoe. I was the ugly and left-out stepdaughter with the wicked stepmom.

The laundry had to be done in a specific method with the towels folded in three, not in two. While vacuuming the carpet, all the lines needed to go in the same direction. As soon as the lines weren't visible on the carpet anymore, it was time to vacuum again. Cleanliness went beyond clean to spotlessness; it had to be pristine. The excessive and unnecessary cleaning was dreadful and burdensome. No matter how well I cleaned, I was still not liked or approved of by my stepmother.

The Truth Hurts

A large quantity of my time was spent being yelled at, being grounded, and listening to lectures which demeaned me and bashed my femininity. I was called names and accused of things I didn't do. According to my parents I was terrible and could do nothing right. I wasn't entitled to any encouragement, praise, or reward. I tried my best to be the daughter they wanted me to be. I tried so hard to be who they wanted me to be, that I had little time to be myself. I was unacceptable to them in many aspects of my being, but the most hurtful way they openly disapproved of me was in regard to my appearance.

Ms. Moose

At fourteen years old, my parents accused me of being fat. My whole family made fun of me for being overweight. Their condemnation of my appearance was expressed on a regular basis. Intriguingly, when I think back and recall what I looked like or see photos, I wasn't fat. I was built differently from them and not skinny.

While sitting at the dinner table and trying to enjoy a peaceful family meal, my stepbrothers made fun of me and called me hurtful names. They "oinked" at me and made other animal noises while I ate and they told coarse jokes to humor each other. They mocked me and called "Miss Piggy." My dad and stepmom sat at the table and giggled along with the boys. They did nothing to stop the taunting that ultimately shattered my heart to pieces and sent me to my room in a sea of tears.

My dad and stepmom yelled at me as I walked across the living room floor. They said I was stomping around and walking too loudly because I was fat. My own parents nicknamed me "Ms. Moose." It was extremely painful to be called names and made fun of by my parents. The pain went deep and sat in my stomach feeling like a bag of heavy rocks weighing me down. Janet took me to a doctor's appointment to have me put on a diet. The physician was a friend of Janet's and told me how healthier and prettier I'd be if I were thin. The doctor put me on a 1200 calorie per day diet and said I should lose ten pounds. He sent me home with pamphlets and a journal to help me count calories. I have no doubt Janet put him up to this.

The morning after my appointment, I woke up with a new mindset about myself and food. I made up my mind that if I were thin, I'd finally make my family accept me. I had obtained knowledge and information to start a new journey and reach an accepted identity. Finally I wouldn't suffer anymore for being fat. With my calorie counter book, a pen in hand, and a will to be thin, I set out to the kitchen for breakfast. Bread was seventy calories a slice. Butter was fifty calories a pat. Jelly was fifty calories a tablespoon. An apple was sixty calories. That should do for breakfast. I read every label and wrote down every bite I ate, meticulously keeping track of all my calories.

Nutrition became my new obsession. I used my lunch periods at school to go to the library and research diets and nutrition. I became infatuated and on a challenging and dangerous adventure to become thin. Frighteningly, this turned into twenty-six years of an eating disorder.

My dad and stepmom were willing to do whatever it took to get me into smaller clothes. They enrolled me in a dance class with high hopes the exercise would help. I attended the dance class not because I wanted to but because they made me. In class I obsessively compared myself to every girl in the room, especially every girl that was prettier and thinner than I was. I began to hate my body and the way I looked. The dance room held many mirrors surrounding me and screaming fat names. The other girls seemed so happy and accepting of themselves. They appeared as if they had no care in the world because they were skinny. There was no way I could compare to them with my thunder thighs, fat rolls, fat face, and flabby arms. My arms were bigger than theirs, and I didn't even have half the strength they did. I continued with the dance class as my parents instructed, and increasingly became more discontent with myself and discouraged at my lack of progress. The dance class didn't help me lose weight. So, my dad had another plan to change my appearance and make me into who he wanted me to be.

Setting the Pace

My dad was discouraged and distraught with me when at first his plans didn't succeed. He must have viewed me in a disgusting manner which deemed me unacceptable to his standards. He kept Junk food off limits to me and placed it up high or hid it. My family made fun of me if I even dared to look at a forbidden Ho-Ho in the pantry. My dad's painful and stinging words shot through my heart as he told me, "I won't have a fat ass daughter around this house." He verbally abused me, ripped out my heart, and stole any inkling of self esteem from my already shallow identity.

My dad punished and humiliated me for being fat. He made me run around our neighborhood block a determined number of times before I could come back home. In the winter, I bundled up in my jacket and hiked through the snow. He watched me from the large bay window of the living room to make sure I followed his instructions while he held a warm cup of coffee in his hand. That makes me seethe with anger thinking about his prideful and haughty self standing there watching me. He ridiculed and humiliated me from a distance, as he sat comfy and cozy in the house and made a fool of me.

If I didn't follow his exercise program, he threatened to take away my hair tools, hair products, and make-up. He knew taking those things away would only make me look and feel uglier leaving me miserable and unwilling to face anyone. Maybe in his mind he had a fantasy of a thin and beautiful daughter. His disappointments were projected onto me and made my life agonizingly painful. Why did I have to pay for his insecurities? My dad's pride wouldn't allow him to be associated with anyone less than perfect, especially his daughter. Perhaps he thought I was ruining his reputation.

Hazardous to your Health

In considerable attempts to encourage me to thinness, my parents gave me exercise videos to follow. Can you say "Jane Fonda"? I spent excessive amounts of time in the basement working on my body rather than somewhere hanging out with friends or even doing homework. I even received an exercise bike for a Christmas gift. They put it in my bedroom at the end of my bed for me to use. I exercised daily, sometimes twice a day and to the point of exhaustion. I became obsessed with exercise and felt non-worthy and non-productive unless I exercised every day.

In high school, my social studies teacher invited me to help manage the boys wrestling team. From this experience, I quickly understood one important factor in boys wrestling: weight is crucial. By watching the boys practice, I learned some weight loss tricks. During practice they often spit into piles of saw dust to lose weight, and they also wore plastic suits to get rid of excess water before a weigh in. At home I copied their irrational behaviors and wrapped myself in large plastic trash bags under my clothes to increase sweat production and I spit into tissues. This was exceptionally dangerous due to the possibility of dehydration, fatigue, electrolyte imbalances, and other complications. I took none of those things into consideration; my only concern was the number on the scale.

Laxatives and appetite suppressants became my daily "vitamins." Laxatives were an ongoing necessity which I eventually became dependent upon daily. The appetite suppressants had undesirable side effects like dizziness, anxiety, strange feelings in my head, and weakness from not eating. I eventually stopped using them after experiencing a rapid heart rate and palpitations which was frightening.

One evening, I watched an educational and informative TV show geared towards teenage girls and bulimia. This show was meant to deter eating disorders and expose its life destroying behaviors. But I was so mentally wounded that I actually found the show inspiring and helpful. It offered me a new diet plan with a fool-proof method for becoming skinny! Becoming bulimic was my new, unfailing means of losing weight and keeping it off.

Fear of being fat consumed me. I lived with an intense fear of being fat and tried to defeat my fear in illogical ways. Fat was a horrible word. Fat was who I was and what everyone thought of me. Fat defined me and made me worthless. I truly believed if I weren't fat, I'd have been loved and accepted by my family. I was too fat to be loved.

18

I am Responsible

I fought hard for the title of daughter instead of "fat ass," the feeling of love instead of rejection, and the words "good job" rather than "run around the block again." The enemy was in my thinking and there was an ongoing war inside my mind. The powers over me were destructive parenting, food, and insecurity. I was stripped of any dignity and left defenseless. My worth was determined by a number on the scale and the mirror constantly told me I looked fat and bloated. I felt terrible about myself and ashamed to be me. The battle and struggle of an eating disorder continued on for years. I drifted through life under a false sense that I was in control by my rules and habits. Shockingly, I'd find out later I was essentially out of control and ruled by distorted thinking.

I humbly admit and accept responsibility for my own actions. I abused my body on my own and wasn't forced to commit my actions. But I also believe my parents were liable for their part. It's unfortunate I lived under the influence of manipulation and control, as well as their ignorance. But in and through it all, I've learned that, "I am more than a conqueror in Christ Jesus." (Romans 8:37)

We must realize we will only heal beyond what we are willing to accept. One of the things I've learned to accept is that I may never receive an apology from the people who are accountable and responsible for their part in my sickness and pain.

It's unbelievable to consider all the things I did while trying to obtain the unachievable "perfect body." My eating disorder truly sent me over the edge and deceived me into thinking I was in control. The list is extensive but some things I did were: simply not eat, restrict and count calories, obsessively exercise, use diuretics, abuse and become addicted to laxatives, took many diet pills, wore ankle weights to burn extra calories, taped plastic garbage bags on my body to sweat off excessive water, binged and purged massive amounts of food, tried many different diets, and more. While I share this, my heart goes out to any of you with an eating disorder. I share your pain. It is real, it hurts, but there is hope!

Please know this: Every human body is flawed. The flaws we don't see in others are covered by make up or clothing, or better yet, airbrushed, or reconstructed by surgery. There is no perfect model body. The only perfection we can have is a heart that's been transformed by Christ Jesus. Transformed and filled with His mercy, grace, and forgiveness. God is perfect; His love for us will fill our needs and emptiness. Don't try another pill or diet. Try Jesus! He works, and I know this from experience.

You must know this truth: you cannot get better on your own! I tried it for years. You need a support group. You need counseling, therapy, or professional help. Some of you will need in-patient treatment. Remember that no matter what it takes, no matter how hard it becomes, keep persevering and keep your eyes on the prize of healing and wholeness. You are worth it! Here is a link to get you started online searching for help: http://www.nationaleatingdisorders.org/find-help-support.

Do not keep your eating disorder a secret. Get help now so you can find healing and freedom from this deadly disease.

Keep Your Chin Up

My smile created dimples which were sweet and intensified my cheek bones. I actually loved my smile and was complimented on it often. However, what my parents saw when they looked at my face was an ugly mole on my chin they viewed as an intense flaw. My mole was an imperfection they refused to tolerate. Truthfully, the mole on my chin never bothered me. It was just part of my face.

At the age of fourteen my dad had this talk with me. "Brooke, you don't want to keep that ugly mole on your chin. No boy will ever want you or love you with that mole. I'm going to take you to the doctor and have it cut off. Trust me; you will thank me someday when you are older!"

It was settled. He made the appointment and took me to the dermatologist. I sat on the cold doctor's table covered in rough paper, staring at a tray of sharp and frightening surgical tools. The doctor came in the room and made small talk with me while he picked up a needle and numbed my chin with a burning injection. After the numbing medication became effective, he sliced off my mole with a sharp blade.

I felt humiliated after the procedure, like I couldn't speak out for my own body. I felt violated. I was only compliant because I wanted to trust my father. I desired love more than anything, especially from my father. I only wanted to please him, and this was just another attempt to earn his love.

As for the part where I was supposed to thank my dad later, he was wrong. It's later, and I realize that when he had my mole cut away, he also cut away part of my self-worth. To me it was never about the mole. It was about wondering why my dad could never love me the way I was. He was always trying to change me into someone or something pleasing in his eyes. He never accepted me for me.

I've been left with some scars you can see and some you can't. I have a slight scar on my chin, but you have to look closely to notice. Over the years, I learned the truth about that mole: I was beautiful with or without it. I'd have found love with or without that mole on my chin. I am now and will always be loved, cherished, and clothed with dignity and respect. That mole on my chin didn't matter. He made it matter.

19

Shamed

*A*t sixteen years of age and in eleventh grade I was young and insecure. I'd often seek attention by looking for love in all the wrong places. I wasn't sleeping around and didn't have an impressive list of boyfriends; I was simply captivated by any attention I received from boys. I wanted to shine and feel important. I wanted to be a "somebody." My minimal self esteem was easily built up or torn down. I was quickly willing to accept and hold tight the small things in my life that brought me a feeling of love and happiness.

Holding a position as one of the managers for the boy's wrestling team; I stayed after school for practices and rode the activity bus home. One evening, on a bus ride home, I was propositioned by a gorgeous, popular guy. Preston was every girl's dream, and I couldn't believe he was even talking to me. He gave me his undivided attention and made me feel special. Preston sat next to me on the bus that evening, and while we rode home in the dark, he pressed his body close to mine and put his arm around me gently, rubbing my back. For a short-lived time he filled a hole and aching desire in my heart. He made a request of me, and I responded inappropriately with "yes." We then engaged in a sexual activity right there on the bus. Desperation and weakness overruled any common sense I had. I was so willing to lose any dignity and self respect for a brief moment of feeling worthy of someone. I was feeling elated with a false sense of love and feelings of being cared for. I fell in love with this feeling I always longed for.

By being with Preston, I expected to become popular at school and make new friends with the "in crowd." Ironically, my expectations were totally crushed when I heard the terrible rumors being spread about me the next day. I quickly became popular, but not in a good way. I was treated with disrespect, frowned upon, and earned names that hurt me deeply. The whole situation became a disaster, and I certainly didn't feel good about the way people looked at me or treated me. It seemed I couldn't win no matter what.

My classmates were quick to judge without personally knowing me or my heart. They didn't know the broken and hurting person I was inside or that I acted out for approval and popularity. They didn't know for a brief moment in time, a popular guy in school made me feel special and good about myself. And they certainly didn't know how deeply disgusted and sick I felt when I got off the bus the night it happened. Knowing I couldn't turn back and change what occurred only left me feeling more broken and hurt. I was wrecked, feeling empty, and painfully living with the ongoing consequences of my actions.

The indecent proposal and my behavior led to even worse consequences than I could've imagined. My stepbrother found out what happened on the bus and told my dad. My dad soon became fully aware of his daughter's inappropriate and unacceptable sexual experience.

When I walked in the door from school a couple days later, I was taken by surprise. My dad was standing in the living room with the most infuriated look on his face. He had angry tears in his eyes, and I wasn't prepared for what happened next.

My dad blasted me with accusations, screamed, and called me names that were unfitting for anyone's daughter. The situation became intense. He quickly lost any bit of self control. I became trapped in my bedroom while he stood there blocking the doorway. He hit me in the face, and I was knocked to the floor. It all happened so fast that when it was over I was distraught, badly hurting physically and emotionally, and had a mark on my face. After I was able to stop sobbing I got up to look in a mirror and saw the red and swollen eye he gave me. He left my room in intense anger without a bit of remorse that night or ever offering an apology.

This was devastating to say the least. I couldn't understand why my dad would hurt me like that. I was overwhelmed with negative emotions and pain I didn't know how to comprehend. I didn't want to live anymore, but I knew suicide wasn't something I wanted to follow through with. I was desperate for all of my pain to go away. I hurt so badly, and I had no one to help me. I just kept thinking, "Why me?"

Yes, I had done something terribly wrong, but I could've used some help or counsel instead of that mistreatment. Why didn't anyone understand me? After deep thinking and self coaching I remembered the promise I made to myself. I wanted protection and freedom from emotional pain and violence. Why did everyone think it was okay to hit and hurt me? I was so confused and vulnerable. I wanted out and away from that man who was called "Dad."

The next morning I made a decision to use the only resource available to me. With a weary mind and trembling hands, I went to my school counselor for help. I waited in the office unsure of what would or could happen next. I only had in mind my own best interest and wanted a change for my life. I was desperate and wanted some immediate help.

The school secretary instructed me to have a seat in a big black chair across from the desk where my school counselor sat. After he came in, I gave him details from my past and enlightened him with my current situation at home. I wanted him to know the pain I was living. The scenario was best painted to him by the colorful river of tears I cried and the black eye I wore on my face. I was honest and explained the event that took place on the bus. I made him aware of my dad's reaction and physical abuse.

My school counselor appeared concerned listening intently while writing everything down on a notepad. He told me someone would look into things more thoroughly but until I heard or knew otherwise, I had to go back home. Sadly disappointed, I went back home to be grounded for an indefinite period of time. No one at home would speak to me and my dad took my bedroom door off the hinges for punishment. He told me I didn't deserve privacy, so I wasn't allowed any. I wasn't permitted to come out of my room except for food and to use the bathroom. I had no desire to communicate with anyone, anyway. I was depressed and couldn't take anymore.

A few short days later, I was unaware we were about to be paid an unexpected visit from social services. This visit didn't go well. My dad and stepmom were appalled I ever went to the school counselor. After social services left, I was verbally attacked by my dad and stepmom. They called me ugly names and flat out told me they didn't want me living in their home. They said they never wanted me there and they wished I never would have come. My stepmom aimed straight for my heart when she spoke these explicit words to me: "I now see why even your own mother never wanted you." To even write these words at this moment still hurts my heart.

Drained, anxious and hopeless I went to my room. I decided I couldn't take it, and I didn't want to live with them anymore. It was clearly evident I didn't belong there. I was left without a choice but to run away and find somewhere else to live. I wasn't sure what was next, but I packed some things and snuck out to my best friend's house where I talked to her and her family. They empathized with me and shared a plan they had been thinking on for some time. They said they knew this day coming, and they were prepared to help me. My friend Samantha asked her parents if I could live with them and they said, "Yes."

20
Samantha's Home

$\mathcal{F}$earful and confused I wouldn't dare call my dad, nor did I even want to speak to him ever again. Samantha's mom called him to say I was safe, and to let him know I was only two blocks away. They talked on the phone for quite some time as I paced back and forth. She told him she wanted to do whatever she could to help and offered me a place to live. Samantha's mom truly knew my circumstances and state of mind. She wanted to nurture and help me.

Without hesitation, my dad and stepmom let me pack my clothes and live with Samantha. The next day as I packed, I could take nothing except my clothes and personal toiletries. My dad wrote a note on a piece of notebook paper and signed it. The note said he was allowing me to live at Samantha's residence and agreed to pay her mom forty dollars a week for expenses. He followed through with paying her for a short period of time, but soon the checks stopped coming.

Shortly after I moved in with Samantha, my dad decided to release all responsibility and liability from himself to me as a parent. At the age of seventeen I was legally emancipated.

An enormous rush of relief came over me after I moved in with Samantha. I was liberated to be myself, free from verbal and physical harm and relieved from constant stress and unreachable demands. Samantha's parents were gracious and kind giving me a home, my own room, and treating me with love as part of their family.

My new living arrangement worked perfectly, and I adjusted quickly. This time was different, though, because it made an enormous difference in my life: I felt wanted and cared about. I didn't have to earn anyone's love or acceptance; it was freely given to me. I agreed to rules for curfew times, cleaning up after myself, obeying Samantha's parents, and the normal household matters. I wasn't living under condemnation all the time. They were reasonable people who wanted to help a teenager find her way in life. They were able to see the best in me and encouraged me to be successful.

Samantha and I had amazing times together. We went shopping, took many trips to the beach, and stayed up late gazing at the stars. We went to the movies, went to school together, and shared life. I was included in Samantha's family and extended family events including holidays. Everyone welcomed me with warm greetings and open arms.

Although I occasionally smoked cigarettes, I never drank alcohol, used drugs, or got involved in any illegal activity. I worked at a fast food restaurant as a cashier to help pay for my basic needs. I received food stamps from the government as well as medical and dental care. Samantha's parents were gracious with their time and resources. They drove me to and from work and helped pay for my first used car. They provided me with clothing, food, and other necessities. They treated me as their own daughter.

While enjoying my new family and my new found freedom, I still had memories and emotions to work through. The ones that caused the most pain were rejection and abandonment. After I moved in with Samantha, neither my dad nor my stepmom contacted or reached out to me again. There was no effort on their part to restore our relationship. No one called to ask how I was doing. The pain was agonizing, and I couldn't comprehend how my dad lived only two blocks away, yet stayed so far from me.

Brisk walking was a tool I used to relieve stress. I loved taking long walks in the neighborhood. Numerous times I watched my dad drive by me in his truck. He looked right at me without showing one ounce of concern or taking a second to wave. Hurt and rejection welled up in me every time. I lived with that pain until time, or food, drove it away. That one question always plagued my heart: Does he even care about me?

While I lived at Samantha's, I celebrated and attended my eleventh grade homecoming, my senior year prom, and my high school graduation. Samantha and the love of her parents were incredibly uplifting and supportive. But inside my heart, it still hurt not to have my own parents there.

Through the chaos, exhaustion, and affliction I was thankful for my sweet and loyal friend, Samantha. She was a life saving God-send who was always there for me. Samantha and her family reached out to me in extraordinary ways; there's no way to ever repay them. Samantha was beautiful inside and out, she encouraged me in good times and bad, and she and her family modeled true family values I desperately needed to experience.

Samantha and I called ourselves "sisters." We are still special to each other today. We trusted each other with secrets and shared our lives together. I was blessed to become so closely involved with her and her family.

Samantha's home and family were attractive and captivating. There was a sweet fragrance of love in the air and an array of smiling faces. While I knew her family wasn't perfect, I also knew they were genuine. Her home was comfortable and hospitable. Her family radiated love. For these people in my life, I'm forever grateful!

21
Future Plans

*E*ver since I was a young child, I was fascinated by doctor's offices, hospitals, medical shows, and medical equipment. The summer I was fourteen years old, I volunteered as a candy striper in a hospital. During that time with every step I took down the hospital hallway and with every pitcher of ice water I poured, I knew without a doubt I wanted to be a nurse. I anticipated and highly esteemed helping people. I loved supporting them with authentic compassion. I had a desire to spend my life making a career of helping people, and I was willing to make that commitment. It was truly a desire in my heart.

My senior year in high school was intense and full of future considerations. I was ecstatic to turn eighteen, eager to graduate, and inspired to enroll into nursing school. I wanted to attend college but that option wasn't available. I didn't have the money for college, I had no car (after totaling mine), and my time was limited living in Samantha's home. I knew I couldn't live there forever, and the thought of them tiring of me caused fear and a yearning to make things happen quickly.

My prayers were answered when I discovered an area nursing school which offered a full-time program. My plan was to graduate, secure a job, and move out on my own to support myself. I eagerly pursued the nursing program and applied for admission. After I registered, I took the necessary tests and waited for the results to determine my future.

While awaiting my test results I graduated my senior year in high school. I was elated, relieved, and uneasy all at the same time. High school graduation was a huge ordeal in our area with around five hundred twenty seniors graduating from my school alone. Our graduation was held in the city coliseum to provide room for everyone.

Graduating was a significant and huge accomplishment. I finally made it. When my name was called out in that huge coliseum and echoed against the walls, I proudly stood up with tears flowing down my cheeks and walked onto the stage to receive my diploma. I had secretly hoped for my dad and stepmom to be seated somewhere in the crowd watching me and cheering me on. Regardless, I still had a smile on my face, a diploma in my hand, and an awesome future ahead of me. (And no, my parents weren't there.)

Next, the long awaited acceptance letter to nursing school finally arrived in the mail. It was uplifting and encouraging to my soul. It made me feel so alive and rejuvenated, giving me a purpose for my future.

Wild at Heart

There was a four-month gap after my high school graduation before the start of nursing school. During this time I held a couple different jobs and had a couple different boyfriends. The money helped me pay for some of nursing school and buy a car. The boyfriends were challenging. I was dating two guys at the same time, and they were best friends: Justin and Brad. I started dating Justin during my senior year in high school; Brad and I started dating in the summer after our senior year.

Justin and I met at work where we were both cashiers. He took an interest in me and my insecurities manipulated my decision to jump head first into a relationship I didn't even want. I wasn't interested in Justin at first. I was charmed by his interest in me. I craved and adored the attention he gave me because it made me feel flattered and special. We dated for almost one year and became deeply involved. At the age of eighteen, we got engaged and planned to marry. We were so young to be engaged, but his insecurities were as deep as my own, and he enjoyed my company and the attention he received as well. We didn't have specific wedding plans, just a proposal and a ring on my finger.

Justin ended up being a jerk. He was selfish and into life for whatever fun, entertainment, and success he could acquire. Everything we did needed to be about him. Anything I asked him to do for me was a huge inconvenience. He wouldn't run to the store for me if I was sick. Justin wasn't emotionally supportive in my times of distress. He was too prideful to say he was ever sorry. And he always wanted sex. I tired of his attitude and behavior quickly but had no one else. Well, until I met his friend, Brad.

Brad was tall with glasses and had dark brown hair. He was intelligent, sweet, and had a slight arrogance but with a care free "go with the flow" attitude I was attracted to. I was in the opposite sense an uptight personality with an anxious and stressful mindset, always worrying about something. But I was fun, loving, outgoing, and enjoyed laughing. We were complete opposites. He was introverted but possessed qualities of strength and logic that were extremely striking. I admired Brad for his self confidence and honest character. I couldn't keep my eyes or mind off him and I began having intense feelings for him the more we all hung out together. One major problem was that I was still engaged to Justin.

I was filled with such intense feelings for Brad that I wanted to explode with euphoria. I could push the feelings away and deny myself the privilege of Brad, or I could risk everything and make Brad aware of my feelings for him. I was hesitant and fearful of the outcome, but I was willing to do whatever necessary to see if Brad felt anything for me. So, I put myself out there and risked it all by telling Brad my feelings for him. I was elated when Brad said he was also attracted to me. However, he was reluctant for us to date or have a relationship, because I was dating his best friend. It was a literal mess. So, we started dating in secret.

Leading a "double life," I continued dating Justin and Brad at the same time to avoid the damaging effect a "break up" would create. I was also scared and embarrassed to reveal my relationship with Brad. I didn't want to hurt Justin or ruin their friendship. I didn't want them to choose each other over me and be stuck with no one. I didn't want to lose Brad because he was the best thing in my entire life that ever happened to me. I was too vulnerable and scared to handle any more negative emotions. And I didn't even know how to deal or handle any of what was going on.

Our love triangle went on for a few months. It became a thrilling ride of two opposing forces: right vs. wrong. My heart and mind were constantly at battle, but I carried on without regard to any consequences. Brad and I were discrete and hid our relationship from everyone. The seriousness of our bond became problematic right as Brad was preparing to leave for college. He was accepted into a respected college in New York which made everything even more complicated. He was about to go off to college and leave me.

Brad and I had some serious conversations and agreed neither of us had any intentions of letting each other go, so we decided to become an "official couple." After Brad left for college, the situation was mine to handle. I broke up with Justin over the phone and told him we had to end our engagement. I'm not sure if my intention was to be honest with Justin so I could clear the air or if I only wanted to tell Justin the truth to help relieve my guilt. I was held hostage to guilt for so long that I needed to be emotionally released from it. Either way, I told Justin the truth but unfortunately it didn't go over well. I crushed him emotionally, broke his heart, and shattered his self esteem. Honestly, breaking his heart also broke mine.

Through the heartache, tears and pain I was still confident knowing the decision I made was for the best. I had no regrets in choosing Brad. The only regret I lived with for years was hurting Justin. Although I got what I wanted in the end, that whole event in my life was a nightmare of confusion, despondency, and pain. I suffered with anxiety, depression, severe panic attacks, and emotional distress. This totally drained and weakened my physical and spiritual well-being. I believe it set me up for what happened to me next: I acquired a rare medical condition.

22

Priorities

ad I made my relationship with Jesus the first priority in my life, this relational travesty may have been prevented. I'd have been seeking Jesus and not guys. I'd have known I was a daughter of the most High King, and I didn't need a guy to fulfill my needs. I wouldn't have kept committing sins over and over just to wake up the next day, say "I am sorry" to God, ask for forgiveness, and then do it over again. Had I submitted myself to the obedience of Jesus, listened for His voice and lived His ways, these shameful events may have been avoided.

We have been given the gift of life to live with exuberant joy and live it to the fullest. But some of us have things seriously wrong in our hearts like I did, and we keep doing what we know is wrong. Some of us keep putting off what we know is important and choosing to live life in our own ways. We need to rethink our priorities and take a deep look within our hearts.

Take a moment to consider what your relationship with Jesus looks like. Is He your friend? Do you communicate with Him on a daily basis? Do you know how much He cares for you? Are you obedient to His word and ways?

You are not reading this by chance or accident. God has a plan and purpose for you. "For I know the plans I have for you," says the LORD. "They are plans for good and not for disaster, to give you a future and a hope." (Jeremiah 29:11)

God's love is extravagant, amazing and available to all. He says, "Come to me, all of you who are weary and carry heavy burdens, and I will give you rest. Take my yoke upon you. Let me teach you, because I am humble and gentle at heart, and you will find rest for your souls. For my yoke is easy and my burden is light." (Matthew 11:28-30)

Ask God to show you ways to develop a deeper and more intimate relationship with Him. He will be overjoyed to answer your prayers.

Losing Sight

Brad and I succeeded in surviving a long distance relationship. We kept in close contact daily over the phone, by letters, and occasional visits. Our time apart was especially hard for me, because I felt incomplete and unloved without him. Brad was my knight in shining armor and the man of my dreams. He held me together when I fell to pieces and helped me see things with a positive mindset.

During that holiday season I prepared to begin nursing school. Life for me was finally taking a turn for the good. One evening, friends and I gathered together for fun and had a whipped cream fight. Oddly that night I got a sudden onset of sharp pain in my right eye. Over the next few days the pain intensified and various symptoms occurred. I was seeing flashes of light, colors grew dim, and there was a dark spot I was seeing in my peripheral vision. I was utterly scared to death. I quickly went to my family doctor. After an exam, the first diagnosis he gave me was "hysterical blindness." It still upsets me for allowing that diagnosis to sit with me for a few days. I was highly anxious, stressed out, and had seen that same physician for heart palpitations. He must have taken all those things into consideration and wrote me off as crazy! Of course I was hysterical; I was slowly losing my vision with severe eye pain.

As my vision grew worse I found an ophthalmologist. He examined my eyes and gave me a diagnosis of eye flu. He put me on a couple eye drops including an antibiotic. I believed this doctor knew best since he was a specialist, but what did I know? I was only eighteen years old. Over a couple weeks I was slowly losing my vision, literally going blind in my right eye. It was a frightening time for me to be without any family or support. I was misdiagnosed several times, lacked medical knowledge, and was scared for my life while feeling like everyone thought I was crazy.

My vision continued to get worse while no one could figure out the cause. I lost all my peripheral vision in the right eye and had almost gone completely blind. In desperation I took myself to the ER. The ER physician called in a neurologist for a consultation. After my exam the doctor admitted me into the hospital with a diagnosis of optic neuritis and placed me on high doses of IV steroids. The neurologist told me he suspected I had Multiple Sclerosis. My next tests consisted of a brain MRI, two excruciatingly painful spinal taps, a brain EEG, blood work, and an Evoked Potential Test. I awaited the results in severe fear and felt hopeless inside anticipating bad news. I was all alone, I had no one with me, and I was scared. Many thoughts went through my head. I envisioned myself in a wheelchair with nothing to live for. It was during this time I sought the Lord like never before. I prayed and begged God not to let me have MS. I made promises to God and bargained with him, promising never to have sex again until I was married.

A couple days into my hospital stay I finally got the test results from the neurologist. My MRI results were normal as well as all my other tests. I was immeasurably relieved of great distress, and I was extremely grateful and thankful to God. I spent the next two weeks in the hospital on IV steroids and other medications. Miraculously, and I do mean miraculously, I got my vision back. Surprised by my recovery, the neurologist said I received treatment just in time to prevent permanent blindness.

These unforeseen and unfortunate events marked a pivotal point in my life. I continued in prayer, reading the bible and seeking God with passion and purpose. A pastor came to visit me in the hospital. He prayed for me and left a pamphlet of prayers on healing. I held those prayers dear to my heart and prayed fervently for complete healing from optic neuritis. When I finally left the hospital I had a severe migraine headache from the spinal taps, but thankfully I regained 100% of my vision. I can now tell you from personal experience that God does listen and answers our prayers. God is a miracle working God. God healed me!

Spiritual Insight

Until then, I had known of God and about God. I had prayed and hoped if I were to die I'd go to heaven. I remembered all I learned when I was a young child in church. But through the devastation, loss, pain, and desperation, God became more real to me. God was calling me to a deep and personal relationship with Him. He wanted me to hand over my heart and trust Him with every part of my life. God showed me that I was never alone, He never left my side, and He was all I truly needed. Praise God for His faithfulness!

God used my situation as a defining moment. I was able to clearly recognize my sins and see how wrong I was living. I prayed and dedicated my life to Jesus and asked Him to help me live as He wanted. I knew He had great plans for me, but they couldn't be accomplished until I stopped trying to control everything in my own power. I didn't understand the amazing plans God had for me and the astounding purpose He created me to accomplish for His glory.

On Sundays I started attending church where God perfectly positioned me to meet some Christian friends. My new friends mentored me by teaching me about Jesus, His ways, and His love. I was baptized in the Holy Spirit and God gave me the gift of speaking in tongues. I began a new journey in my life with exuberant joy and hope. Prayer is powerful and it's beneficial to our well-being to live in constant communication with God. Prayer moves the heart and hand of God, prayer reaches the heart and throne room of God. Prayer is like breathing: a necessity for living.

Living on a Prayer

Prayer isn't a magical formula or words of repetition. Prayer is communication with God, talking to Him and sharing our hearts. Listening to Him and waiting for His response. Our prayers change impossible situations because, "with God all things are possible." (Matthew 19:26) "It's the prayers of the righteous that avail much." (James 5:16) Prayers of faith fully expectant on God alone, move the hand of God to do the miraculous, and bring him glory and honor. Prayer is so powerful; our prayers are eternal.

Prayers are spoken in many languages, tongues, groaning and utterances, and then interpreted by our heavenly Father. The throne room of God is rocked with thunderous sounds which reveal the power of the Holy Spirit whom indwell in our prayers. Prayer spoken in faith brings the dead back to life and heals the sick and the blind. Prayer keeps us alive, fills us with hope, and brings change and deliverance. Prayer reveals the awesomeness of God, conveys revelation and supplies us with God's wisdom. God gives us insight into the spiritual realm and the ability to recognize and realize our battle is not one dimension.

"For we are not fighting against flesh-and-blood enemies, but against evil rulers and authorities of the unseen world, against mighty powers in this dark world, and against evil spirits in the heavenly places." (Ephesians 6:12)

In this life, prayer is not an option but it's a daily necessity. You will accomplish more in minutes with God's power than you can accomplish on your own, in your lifetime. Whatever we want, whatever we desire, in whatever we do, we must pray. Prayer allows God to search our hearts, transform us into his likeness and miraculously change situations so everything can be used for His glory.

If you want to live a life victorious, see impossible change, and better understand God's will and purpose for you; you must pray! Pray with expectancy, pray without doubt, and trust that God hears every word, spoken and unspoken. Our faith is not in prayer itself, but our faith is in God our Creator in whom we can trust with our lives.

23
New Hope

Nursing school was tough, but it was an amazing year spent pursuing my dream. Brad and I continued dating and growing in our friendship while he kept up with college. This time was challenging while we wrestled with maintaining focus on our studies and balancing our relationship.

Samantha left for college, and her parents graciously allowed me to stay in their home. In anticipation of my nursing graduation, I mentally began to prepare for my future job and a new home. I knew I couldn't survive financially single. Brad and I decided that when I graduated nursing school I'd move to New York City with him, and we could share an apartment. Although it did make sense financially, we both knew it wasn't going to be acceptable to his parents because they were "old fashioned" and protective of Brad. I personally knew it wasn't a good "Christian" choice to make, but I was desperate for security and independence.

Feelings of honor, joy, and relief filled me as I received my hard earned diploma from nursing school. I stepped onto the stage and accepted my diploma with a bigger smile on my face and in my heart than ever before. I had support from my classmates and teachers, but once again I celebrated another major life accomplishment without family. Even Brad was unable to attend my graduation. I chose to focus on the positive outcome and new beginnings but it still hurt.

Two days after graduation I packed all my clothes into the back of my white Reliant K-car and without looking back or hesitation, I left for New York City. I happily anticipated the new beginning of a remarkable future with Brad. My heart was content and full of glorious hope. Cheers to new beginnings.

City Life

Brad and I rented a small, one bedroom apartment as I started my first job as a nurse at a city hospital. Brad continued college classes. Together, we were enjoying the awesomeness of our relationship. Finally, we were together, just the two of us!

About six weeks after we were moved in together, I undoubtingly knew God was speaking to my heart. My spirit was awakened and my thinking enlightened as God convicted me of the constant sin of pre-marital sex. In my mind I rationalized the reason we lived together, however I was not able to rationalize the sin of sleeping together.

Unfortunately, rather than having a pure heart and wanting to obey God out of love and being submissive, I was ruled by fear. The fear of getting pregnant consumed me. I couldn't shake the guilt and fear. I shared my convictions and feelings with Brad. Finally, I made a decision to stop having sex with him until we were married. We agreed it would be difficult, but it could be done.

The shocking irony of my decision was revealed just two weeks later. I found out I was pregnant. This riveting news shook us dramatically and challenged our relationship and our lives. We were forced to make life altering changes which were difficult to initiate and rise above. We had to quickly mature and endure a hard lesson in learning to put something or should I say "someone" above ourselves. Brad had to swallow his pride and eventually confront his parents with the news of my pregnancy. This took him four months. While they weren't enthusiastic, they were vastly supportive.

Painful Acceptance

My heart was troubled. I truly believed I got pregnant because God was punishing me for my sin. My whole world felt like it was crashing into ruins. The thought of having an abortion crossed my mind as a way out of my despair. Brad was adamant he didn't want me to have an abortion nor would he allow me to consider one. I was exceptionally grateful for his support, and I felt better knowing I was not without him. It was an upsetting and intimidating feeling to have just turned twenty years old, not married, and pregnant. It would have been so easy for Brad to walk out on me and say his farewell. Thankfully, he accepted responsibility and stayed by my side.

Being pregnant, I felt it would only be fair to let my parents know they had a grandchild on the way. It took some time and energy, but with persistence, I located my mother who was still living in New Mexico. After seven years of separation, we spoke for the first time. She was elated to hear from me and excited to become a grandma for the first time. We reconnected verbally, but there was no relationship to rekindle. I accepted it as a new season to start over with her and truly forgive for all the pain she caused.

My dad still lived in his same house, having his same phone number, making him easy to find. It was difficult to pick up the phone and call my dad. I was still emotionally hurting from our past. I prepared my heart for the worst case scenario which included more rejection from him. My intention was to be fair by informing my dad he would be a grandpa. I was also open and willing to move forward with him in a relationship if the opportunity presented itself.

My dad was taken by surprise with my phone call. I was surprised he even spoke to me after he heard my voice. He accepted the news with excitement and asked to meet with Brad and me. A couple weeks later we traveled to visit my dad and stepmom so they could meet Brad and we could re-connect. This was an awkward time to say the least but we moved forward for the sake of restoration and a new baby on the way.

My dad and stepmom were the same people they'd always been. They showed no regret and didn't offer an apology for anything in the past. But I decided to accept them as they were and forgive them anyway; there was no room for bitterness in my heart. I wasn't able to realize it at the time, but I was still living with a deep and desperate need to be loved and accepted by my dad.

It's a Boy

We delivered our healthy 8 pound 10 ounce baby boy on a cold January night in the city hospital. Holding that precious baby in my arms was a life changing experience I will never forget. I held something so dear, tender and precious. I named him Matthew, called him my own, and was able to love him in a meaningful and nurturing way. In that delivery room, I realized our son was a gift from God; he was an extravagant blessing rather than a punishment for my sin.

Our options were limited after Matthew's birth. It wasn't financially feasible for Brad to continue college while I worked full time and also pay for child care. We had no family or friends to help us. Brad's parents asked us to move back home and stay with them until we found a place of our own. They promised to help with the baby and watch him so we wouldn't need to pay child care.

Brad quit college, I quit my job, and we packed up a U-Haul with our newborn baby and moved back to our hometown in New York. Moving was a wise choice but far from a simple decision. We struggled with wanting to maintain independence and also feeling dependent upon our parents.

We settled in with my in laws, but right away, we started looking for our own place. God blessed me greatly with a job at a local hospital. Brad worked a part time job at a home improvement store while attending a university off-site campus. Six weeks later, we happily moved into our own mobile home. It was small but nice, and finally a place to call our own.

For only twenty-one years of age, we were responsible and made excellent parents. Our home was kept clean, the laundry always done, and I took delight in maintaining the inside of our home. Brad took care of the vehicles, grew a garden, and did more than I could ever have asked from him.

Despite our circumstances, my heart was constantly burdened. We weren't married but portrayed the false image of a married couple. While I wanted to get married, Brad wasn't on board with the idea. He reasoned that he wanted to be financially stable before he made that commitment. Sometimes, I felt his response was just a cop-out to cover his uncertainty.

We had some problems in our relationship with communication and our behavior. Our attitudes and actions towards each other weren't always pleasant or kind. Brad could be angry, critical, and distant. I was manipulative, disrespectful, and out of control with my mouth and my emotions. We did our best to make things work day to day, but neither of us was humble enough to change or admit our wrongs.

In an attempt to seek God and His help, I started going to an Assembly of God church on Sundays. Brad was apprehensive about going to a church that wasn't Catholic. He spent his childhood attending a Catholic church and school. I didn't want to attend a Catholic church. I had tried them before and didn't enjoy the experience or learn when I was there. It wasn't for me; I personally enjoyed something more charismatic.

I spent time praying and believing in faith, hoping one day Brad would come to church with me. At church on Sunday mornings I'd sing praises to God and tearfully watch other happy families joined together. My heart was sad and I desperately wanted my own family to attend church and share the same experiences.

It took approximately six months of fervent prayer before Brad decided to try the church with me. It was like a warm cup of soothing tea for my soul when we went to church for the first time as a family. It was nothing less than answered prayer. Brad and I sat in the sanctuary while Matthew went to the lovely nursery they provided. Shortly after we began attending church together, God started working more in our hearts. We became sensitive to God's prompting and allowed Him to make changes within us to better ourselves and our relationship. Our eyes were opened in incredible ways and we were able to view things from God's perspective by hearing His word. We became more perceptive, hearing Him speak to our hearts.

I Do

Brad proposed to me on a cool, windy day at the beach. He got down on one knee in the sand and with a gorgeous diamond ring in his hand, he properly asked me to marry him. Without hesitation my answer was, "Yes!"

It didn't take long to plan our wedding. We had little money and a small family to invite. Our obstacles were overcome by determination and flexibility. We had no money to buy my wedding dress, so we compromised. I located a shop in town that rented dresses. For ninety-nine dollars, I rented a dress with a return policy for the day after the wedding. Our initial wedding day was a Saturday, but due to the reception hall availability, it had to be moved to a Sunday.

We were married in May on a record-breaking day with temps rising to 100 degrees. We drove ninety minutes away to the church where we were married. The pastor was a friend of the family's who performed our wedding on a Sunday. We stood in a small country church with no air conditioning, just a standing fan blowing on our faces. We exchanged our wedding vows in front of about fifty people. Perspiration and make-up ran down my face along with my tears as I recited my vows and then accidently placed Brad's ring on his wrong hand. It was an embarrassing, but now funny, "wedding blooper" caught on video.

After the wedding we didn't leave in a fancy car or limousine. We drove off in the best man's Camaro. Our reception was pretty normal except someone stepped on the back of my wedding dress and ripped it while we were dancing. Thankfully Brad's mom could sew and did a great job before the return of the rented dress.

Our honeymoon night was extremely interesting. I blame bad manufacturing when the condom broke during our intimate evening. We didn't sleep well that night since we worried about the possibility of a way too early second pregnancy. The next morning we ventured out on our road trip to Myrtle Beach, South Carolina. The ride itself would have been better had our air conditioner in the car not broken. It was almost one-hundred degrees in South Carolina. Thankfully it was broken at the highest cold air setting so we froze instead of roasted. This didn't make for a comfortable ride physically or mentally, as we bickered about the broken air conditioning.

Although our wedding and honeymoon were far from perfect, it created unforgettable memories, and God blessed me with an incredible husband. Through the imperfections I'm reminded of life's journey we travel. We try so hard and struggle to make perfect plans in the hope that things will work out our way. However, we must always remember we have less control than we think. We need to learn to give everything over to God. He can do a better job than we can. Things may not always work out the way we want, but God sees the bigger picture. God will cause everything to work for good. "And we know that God causes everything to work together for the good of those who love God and are called according to his purpose for them."(Romans 8:28)

24
Aim High

oney was tight and times were tough. I worked full time as a nurse while Brad attended college and worked the night shift in a hardware store. Brad was about six months away from graduating college and we anticipated him finding a job and then us finding a house.

We were unprepared and shocked from the unexpected news about Brad's college. Brad was notified his credits from his previous college didn't transfer over correctly. The error was never caught until the most inopportune time; he was one semester away from graduation. Brad was informed he needed another two classes to graduate but these classes wouldn't be offered for another year. It would then take one year longer for Brad to graduate. This wasn't practical for us with our finances and living arrangements. Consequently, we had to start thinking out of the box for a solution to this awful, mind-blowing setback.

Brad thought hard about joining the military and met with a recruiter. He was given information about benefits, college money, and opportunities as well as their promise to take care of his family and needs. After all was said and done, Brad enlisted in the United States Air Force for four years and thus a new voyage began.

Bon Voyage

We were "off into the wild blue yonder." Brad completed boot camp, and then we headed to Goodfellow AFB in Texas for his technical training school.

Brad and I were adapting to our life in the Air Force and ready to receive his new orders. We decided it was time to start trying for our second baby we both wanted. It was only two months later when we got the amazing confirmation, I was pregnant. We didn't plan for it to happen so fast, but God's timing is always best, even when we don't understand it.

Brad received his new orders when I was three months pregnant. We were headed to an Air Force base in Illinois. The Air Force provided us with nice base housing. Impressively we moved into a sweet two-story duplex. It had three bedrooms, two bathrooms, a nice front yard, large back yard, and a car port. It was by far the nicest place we had lived in yet. We were upgraded from a tiny apartment to a mobile home and now to a nice duplex with lots of room for our family.

My first experience in Illinois was unforgettable as I encountered intense winds. Upon our arrival I stepped out of our car into a McDonald's parking lot for lunch and found myself clinging onto the door as my hair blew wildly out of control and I watched papers flying everywhere. It wasn't a wind storm but in fact Illinois' normal spring weather. We eventually settled in and accepted the cornfields, wind, flat land and being in the middle of nowhere. This was our new home for the next three and a half years.

Brad became established in his position working on computers. He worked an unbelievable job Monday through Friday with the rare event of being "on call." He was never sent out of the country, and we were well taken care of by the amenities of the Air Force. He enrolled in a local college and after hard work and determination; he earned his bachelor's degree.

In August of 1998 our beautiful daughter, Abby was born in Illinois. Abby was a miraculous addition to our family, and we simply adored her. Matthew was accepting of his new little sister and with a twinkle in his eye and a huge grin on his face, he held her for the first time in the hospital. With one boy and one girl, our family was perfectly complete, and we were absolutely content.

Heart Transformation

Our family started attending a Southern Baptist Church in Illinois. The church was large and held around three-thousand members. We were extremely impressed with the pastor and the biblical messages he spoke which touched our hearts with truth and significant meaning. After two visits we knew it was our new church. We stayed committed and called it our home church for three and a half years.

It was during these incredible three and a half years God did an astounding work in our hearts and marriage. Brad gave his life whole heartedly to Jesus and was water baptized. I attended several women's Bible studies that drew me closer to God. The Lord continued to change us. I learned a great deal about living as a Christian and being a godly woman. I was introduced to prayer on a deeper level during a seminar and challenged to be a prayer warrior. I shed countless tears, learned many lessons, picked up broken pieces of my heart off the floor as well as battled with God over obedience to Him. All I can say is "Wow!" It was a total life transformation for me, not at all easy, but I'd never give back one moment. I wouldn't be who I am today if I had not gone through it all.

While we lived in Illinois, life was good. God provided all our needs and kept us safe and healthy. We learned to be a family and went on many trips to the zoo, parks, malls, and on a few great vacations. Brad and I continued to mature as Christians while God drew us closer to His heart and to each other.

When it was time for Brad to reenlist in the Air Force after his four years were almost over, he made the decision to separate. He had prayed about this choice and knew it was in the best interest for all of us. Ironically, Brad received intelligence telling him he had new orders to depart to Korea for one year, but considering he wasn't reenlisting they were cancelled. My heart skipped several beats upon hearing the news and I was extremely thankful. I can't imagine to this day how I'd have made it with two small children and no husband or daddy around.

Journey of Faith

Time grew near for Brad to separate from the military. We prayed desperate and fervent prayers for guidance. We had no idea where we were going or where we would live or work. Holding a bachelor's degree, Brad sent out hundreds of resumes around the country searching for a job. Brad was ready and willing to take whatever was offered. Ironically, we both had the desire to move to Washington DC. The capitol sounded like an exciting place to live with its pretty scenery and mild climate. We were in agreement and prayed for our new home.

Without a word from the job market and time closing in on us, Brad received a surprising call from a distant friend. His friend Alex had recently made a visit to Washington DC for a job interview and held the same degree as Brad. We had no idea whatsoever that this friend was looking for a new job. The job and location didn't suit Alex's lifestyle so when he declined the offer they asked for any personal referrals and he gave them Brad's information. We were exceptionally grateful and flabbergasted after hearing this news.

A couple weeks later, Brad received a phone call and was asked to fly to Washington DC for a job interview. The company paid for all Brad's travel and hotel expenses. The whole process took about six weeks which consisted of two interviews, paperwork, and more. Then one afternoon when I walked in the door with the kids after running errands, I pushed the play button on the answering machine. There was a message for Brad regarding his new job and special congratulations. I still remember the extreme joy and ecstatic energy I felt as I ran around the house screaming with thankfulness. I was more than grateful and highly impressed with God's impeccable timing and willingness to answer prayer. This was an overwhelming situation in our lives and certainly a lesson on trust and faith in God. So as it was, we would soon be off to our new destination in Washington DC.

Intimate Encounter

It's a personal and sometimes indescribable experience to have a close and intimate encounter with Jesus. This is one I will never forget as it lives so vivid in my mind. Closing my eyes in the midst of worship I envisioned myself on the beach with Jesus. We had a picnic on the beach. I spent time sharing with Him my worries and problems. He wasn't a bit amazed at the trials I was going through. Jesus not only listened to me intently, but He had an amazing love and compassion beyond explanation.

When Jesus got up to walk away I remembered the verse in the Bible where a woman touched the hem of His garment in faith believing for healing. I reached out, grabbed the bottom of His robe, and He turned around. I asked Him to please heal me of the disease and pain in my body. Jesus looked at me on the ground and asked me, "Do you want to be healed?" "Yes," I replied. "I want healing. I don't want to live with this constant pain anymore."

On the shore of the beach Jesus and I danced together in the sand. He took my hands, and we spun around in circles laughing and having a wonderful time. Jesus touched my mind and told me it needed to be renewed; then he touched my heart, and I felt an incredible love I never wanted to depart from me. Tears came to my eyes as I asked Him to please never leave me. Jesus reminded me that He will never leave me nor forsake me.

There was a small boat sitting on the water, and Jesus took me for a ride. We went out to a place where the water was still. As I looked around, storms encircled us but none came close. Jesus showed me that in His presence I am kept safe. He then encouraged me to step out of the boat and to walk on the water with Him. I held onto His hand and didn't doubt it was possible because I remembered the story when Peter walked on the water. We stepped out of the boat and, holding His hand, we walked on the water. I then asked Jesus why I was going through trials. His response to me was "to test and prove your faith."

Jesus told me that anyone can speak words out of their mouth, but it does not make them true. When we go through suffering and trust God for what we need, our faith in Him will create a response of action that will prove to others what God will and can do. That will then be used as a testimony of God's amazing grace, mercy, and love.

"So be truly glad. There is wonderful joy ahead, even though you have to endure many trials for a little while. These trials will show your faith is genuine. It is being tested as fire tests and purifies gold—though your faith is far more precious than mere gold. So when your faith remains strong through many trials, it will bring you much praise and glory and honor on the day when Jesus Christ is revealed to the whole world." (1 Peter 1:6-7)

25
Life on the East Coast

We were extremely blessed and provided for with all the means necessary to make this move easy and affordable. The only thing we had to do ourselves was find a place to live. We traveled for two days to reach our destination. Exhausted and excited we all finally arrived to DC and moved into our new townhouse.

Immediately I hunted for a job, interested in a large, gorgeous hospital in the area. I submitted my resume and application with great anticipation for the privilege of a position there. Four weeks later, I was interviewed and employed as a nurse at the hospital I wanted. The pay was good, and I spent most of my time working on the medical floor which was my favorite place. Brad was settling in nicely at his new job, and the kids were happily adjusting.

We both loved our new hometown in Washington DC. Relocating to this area was exhilarating with many grand possibilities of travel adventures and tourism at hand. With all the positives, we had not prepared for or even considered any dangers of our location. This was the month of September and the year 2001.

Almost every one of us can account for and remember where we were and what we were doing on that day. On the morning of September 11, 2001 Brad was at work, and I was at a Bible study in a new church. The news of a plane crashing into the Twin Towers surfaced and spread rapidly among all the women at church. Then the same happened with the news of the Pentagon being hit. Everyone was instructed to remain calm, and we were assured the accident at the Pentagon had caused minimal damage. Many of the women were receiving phone calls from their husbands to alert them and tell them they were okay. I left the church and quickly went over to the hospital to finish paperwork needed for my new job. After arriving at the hospital the news was widespread and terror had struck the area while everything was quickly being tied together and called "terrorist attacks." The fear was intense and it was felt in every one's actions and words. At the hospital the employees were expected to carry out business as usual and keep calm especially for the sake of patients. My papers were quickly processed, and I headed home to be with my family. Brad phoned me and was on his way home after his building was closed for the day.

Who can ever forget the absolute chaos and terror everyone experienced that day? Loved ones were lost from people in our area who worked at the Pentagon. The news constantly played the plane crashes over again with scenes and events from the attacks. While we watched this with pure horror, our hearts were sick with anticipation of another probable attack closer to us. It was certainly a time to remember, a time where people joined together to pray and reach out to each other for support. These events were horribly evil. Only God was able to bring good from them. People's hearts were united, they were spiritually saved, and the outpouring of compassion and unity was beyond fathomable.

Saving Grace

Brad bought his first motorcycle at the age of eighteen. He was well educated in safety and had taken special classes to prepare for riding. He was always cautious and rarely risked traffic violations. When he rode, he wore his helmet, special Kevlar gear, gloves, and boots. Riding a motorcycle was exciting for him and from what I understand it gave him the ability to go from zero to sixty miles per hour in three seconds.

When we moved to Washington DC, he had a special desire to buy a new motorcycle. After some research and shopping, he bought a Suzuki Katana 750. It was a gorgeous bike in silver and black. It dazzled in the sunshine and roared like thunder down the streets. I was fortunate to go on some rides with him, but my desire to live, kept me off that bike many times. It wasn't my aspiration to ride something

I knew was dangerous and without a seatbelt, no matter how much Brad assured me he was a safe driver.

On a gorgeous fall day I kissed Brad goodbye as he headed out the door with his helmet in hand and complete outfit of black gear intact. I continued with my household duties taking care of the kids as on any normal morning. Later in the bathroom, I was preparing to put on my make-up when the phone rang. This was the one dreaded phone call we all prepare ourselves for, but with every bit of hope within us, we pray it will never happen. The caller ID read "Briar Memorial Hospital." My first reaction was a feeling of disappointment and I hesitated to answer the phone. It was my day off and I assumed my boss was calling to ask me to work that evening.

After a few rings I answered, and a woman identified herself as a nurse from the hospital ER. The nurse told me they had my husband who had just been in an accident. My stomach sunk to the floor, my heart filled with anxiety, and tears welled in my eyes. The nurse assured me he was okay, and they were taking good care of him. She asked me to come to the ER, but I didn't believe he could be doing well after a motorcycle accident. I demanded to speak with Brad. The nurse told me he was having x-rays done, and he was unable to talk on the phone. I quickly became agitated and nervous, yelling at the nurse. I told her I was also a nurse, and I knew she was lying to protect me. She reassured me Brad was fine and to drive safely to the hospital.

After I hung up, I phoned a friend and told her about my emergency. She came to my house and volunteered to watch Abby and Matthew so I could go alone to be with Brad. In shock and without acting sensibly, I proceeded to put on my make-up. I decided I wanted to look good for everyone when they told me my husband was dead. I prepared myself the best I was able, and then drove erratically to the hospital.

Bolting through the ER doors, to my greatest dismay, I spotted Brad sitting in the waiting room holding onto a pair of crutches. He looked well for being in a motorcycle accident. He asked me what took so long to get there and told me he had been waiting for me to pick him up for quite a while. Brad had a bruised and swollen ankle and no other injuries to his whole body.

Brad shared the details of the accident with me on our drive home. He had been sitting in a line of traffic on his motorcycle when a car slammed into the back of him, going about thirty miles per hour. The young man in the car at the age of nineteen was looking down at something and not paying attention to notice traffic had stopped. He rear-ended the motorcycle, and Brad flew off the motorcycle. The motorcycle went underneath the car, crunched, and completely totaled. Brad landed in the middle of a road about twenty feet from his motorcycle. He couldn't remember specifics after he hit the ground except hearing the EMS personnel asking him questions and the pain of a huge IV in his arm. His Kevlar was cut off by medics; he was placed on a stretcher and taken by ambulance to the hospital.

Considering the damage to the motorcycle and the events of the accident, it is by the grace of God that Brad only had a sprained ankle and no other injuries. It was simply a miracle he was alive and well. This miracle was well noted and talked about by the medical personnel at the accident scene and at the hospital. That was the last motorcycle Brad has owned, and we don't see another one in the future. Or at least I hope!

26
A Dangerous Time

The year 2002 was an ideal time for us to build our first brand new house. The building materials, land, and fees were low, allowing us to build a gorgeous colonial house in a suburban subdivision. Our house was spacious with three levels, a full basement, two car garages, and a large front and back yard. It was an exciting experience to watch our house being built from start to finish.

Looking in from the outside, our family had it all together. We were living the "American Dream." According to the standards of the world, we did have it all. Unfortunately, had anyone spent a week in our home, strife was evident, and peace was seldom. I was disrespectful to Brad, and he had a bad attitude towards me. There were many days I felt something wasn't right. I became suspicious of Brad. Our schedules were typical as we worked, took care of the kids, ran a home, and went to church on Sundays.

As I grew in my relationship with God, He began to reveal there was a deep, genuine love and respect lacking between Brad and me. The truth is, God loves us so much that He is not willing to let us live in a mediocre fashion while He has a more fulfilling and exciting marriage available for us. He kept pressing my heart and working to get my attention. God was showing me revelation and truth. I was hearing messages at church, reading devotionals, and learning that a godly marriage can only be lived and experienced when we put God first in our lives and in all we do. We have to allow God to be the center of our hearts and our home.

Shaken and Stirred

One year after the 911 terror attacks on our nation's capital we were tormented with the terrifying events of the DC sniper. We lived near to where one of the shootings took place. During the time of these events, the sniper attacks left us and our whole surrounding area in a constant panic. People were frightened to leave their homes for work, to go shopping, or to attend events. Children were kept inside for fear of their lives, and some people were too scared to open their window blinds. It paralyzed many and placed a halt on life. People hid to stay protected.

One of the letters from the sniper declared, "Children were not safe anywhere or at any time." Our local schools spent a day on "lock down" creating an even more intense fear. People were literally running and ducking when they went into stores and hid behind their cars or in their cars while pumping gas. The local news advised the general public to run in a zigzag manner to decrease the likelihood of being struck by a bullet. Some DC area schools closed and canceled field trips and outdoor activities. This was definitely a time when we were encouraged to pray and trust God for our safety. No amount of words I write about this horrifying occasion can express the depth of the reality of terror we experienced.

Intense relief came when the suspects were apprehended. I am so sorry for all the victims, their families, and friends. I can't even comprehend the pain they faced and still live with today. I am grateful more people weren't hurt or killed.

27

Frenemies

*I*n 2004 we found ourselves in a predicament that would change our lives. This journey would take us places down a path we had never dreamed.

We attended a church in our area for a little over a year and found ourselves contently learning and growing as Christians. We reached out to the pastor and his family, had them over for cook-outs and dinners, and went on day trips together sharing our lives.

As our friends, they shared their secrets with us. This included their daunting past and current problems. We then began to witness first hand, the devastating effects on the lives of a pastor and his wife who lived without God first and center. The pastor's wife was an alcoholic destroying her marriage, children, and home. The heartbreaking, stomach-aching events that follow may throw you for a loop or just leave you with your mouth hanging open. So, let me enlighten you to what happens in this real world of "not so perfect." People are not always who you make them out to be. People are not always who you think they are. Everyone has a history and not everyone likes it or is willing to share their stories.

A not-so-perfect past makes us feel dirty, bad, guilty, and vulnerable to judgment and criticism. However, it is the truth that will set us free. The truth helps others know they aren't struggling alone in this world, and we all face the same real life issues. Whether you have been there and done that, know someone who has, or believe you would never do that, you never know what you are capable of until you are faced and placed in the situation. One of life's greatest lessons is learning not to judge others. I ask you to please not judge me as I share my heart with you. It is my mission to help you know you are not alone in the real issues in life we face!

Deception's Direction is Dangerous

My family and I continued to make personal connections with Pastor Aaron and his family. We watched in shock as their fifteen years of marriage deteriorated quickly. Aaron's wife began drinking more and more. This created intense problems for them which included police involvement in their troubles. There was no compassion visible or even an ounce of love noticed between them. They spoke horribly to and about each other. They lived in separate worlds physically and emotionally. Brad and I did our best to help them in ways we could and provided optimal emotional support. My heart broke for Aaron, and I became deeply involved in his problems. I was desperate to help him and his hurting heart. Continuously, Aaron turned to me for advice and support. Brad warned me not to become as involved as I was, but I rebelled against my husband and did what I wanted to without any respect or regard to his requests.

What I'm about to share with you is extremely personal, embarrassing, and humiliating. Aaron and I started flirting and secretly enjoying each other's companionship and friendship. We became emotionally involved talking over the phone, emailing, and planning things so we could spend time together. We didn't admit or talk about what was happening. I pushed guilty thoughts and all conviction to the back of my mind and chose to live in denial. An emotional affair sparked between us, one that carried on for months. And the closer I grew to Aaron, the further I grew from my husband.

In reality, I was looking to another man to meet my needs. My greatest needs since childhood were love and acceptance. I followed my feelings and allowed lying and cheating to lead my actions. I was unable to hear or believe truth or logic. I was living in a deep dark hole of deception. I began to think about and believe the lies in my head. I believed beyond a doubt that God wanted me to leave my husband

and be with Aaron. I envisioned myself as a pastor's wife and the wonderful life we'd share together.

God did His job and warned me many times about my sin. I read it in the Bible, heard it from my friends and God spoke the truth to my heart through conviction. Neglecting truth and the given resources, I chose to ignore God and His wisdom. I persisted in fulfilling my own selfish desires. It seemed every wrong choice I made only put me in a darker place. My marital problems grew worse. I became more stubborn, disrespectful, and detached towards Brad, even denying any love for him. I searched deeply for any reasons I could use to rationalize why Brad and I should divorce. Being with Aaron at any cost became my main goal and focus.

I ran to Aaron for his help with all my marriage problems, sharing deep and personal issues between Brad and me. I trusted and respected him since he was a pastor and had counseled countless couples. I took matters to him privately and also requested his counseling services for my marriage. Aaron spent time with Brad and me listening to our troubles and giving advice. I couldn't see it at the time, but I find it interesting that I wanted help and trusted someone for marriage counsel when their own marriage was chaotic and falling apart.

Obvious Suspicions

My suspicions ran wild for a long time that Brad was keeping secrets from me. Over the years I looked in his wallet, searched his closet, and wondered why he had a private password on our computer. There was a consistent, vague feeling unsettling my heart and causing me to think he was having an affair. However, none of my leads ever produced any evidence.

Nonetheless, our past had an intriguing connection to all my suspicion. When Brad and I were dating we watched pornography and found it exciting and entertaining. After we were married and I grew closer to God those types of movies made me feel outraged and disgusted. I put my foot down and refused to watch pornography or allow it in our home. Brad agreed and we trashed pornographic video tapes.

Even so, after our agreement I'd occasionally find hidden pornography. When I'd confront Brad he was carelessly rude with his responses and made it clear he didn't find it an issue. He appeared unconcerned with my feelings but again would agree to keep it out of our home. Over time we had numerous discussions and fights about pornography and how it clearly affected our minds, our hearts, and the marriage bed. Pornography became a sensitive subject for me. I couldn't understand why Brad wouldn't be more sensitive to my feelings and grasp the destructive issue.

Pornography was my main grievance with Brad. I used this to justify the need for a divorce. I no longer wanted to be with a man who wasn't sensitive to my needs and treated me as an object. This trouble in our marriage gave me more motivation to pursue a relationship with Aaron. I wanted and needed someone who cared and someone to talk to. After all, Aaron promised to make me happy and take care of me.

Without exaggeration and beyond a reasonable doubt, I know that Brad looking at and watching pornography affected his heart and attitude towards me not only as a woman, but as his wife. I was treated as an object instead of a woman who was to be respected and cherished. I felt dirty and used on various occasions and also unable to fulfill his needs as he desired. My husband was being infected with lies of the devil and destructive images were placed in his head.

A short time passed after I gave Brad a warning. It appeared things were better but my suspicions returned. Through prayer, in search of an answer, I was led to our home computer. Somehow and for some reason, Brad stayed logged into the computer before he left for work. My heart sunk into my stomach and anxiety filled my mind as I was given an opportunity to look at Brad's files. Checking the computer's history brought me grief, anger, tears, hurt, rejection, and a mixture of emotions no woman wants to bear. I was devastated, completely broken, betrayed, and feeling unloved. Pornography corrupted our computer and I went into an emotional frenzy.

My reactions that followed were irrational and illogical, but I was unable to see it at the time. Involved in an emotional affair, I was out of touch with God and unable to be reasonable. Finding the pornography gave me more ammunition for the thoughts and feelings I already struggled with. At the end of my rope, I decided our marriage was over. I tried to reason with myself in many ways to get what I wanted.

I determined I had someone else in my life that would take care of me and never treat or hurt me like Brad. I didn't need more convincing that I was supposed to leave my husband and be with Aaron. I was an extremist, and my mind was made up.

Aaron's problems, faults, or even his own marital issues were not something I took into consideration. All I saw and felt was something different and better in someone else. With one wrong choice after another, I continued with foolish decisions. I spent time reading my Bible and looking for answers to suit my own thinking, seeking the opinions and advice of others. People I trusted and turned to led me in the wrong direction. I created lies and made Brad out to be a terrible monster that was abusive and unbearable to live with. I needed to do all these things so everything would appear to be in my favor.

Due to anxiety and depression I was barely able to function. I was so confused. My life was spinning out of control. I decided to make permanent changes so things would go the way I wanted. I gave Brad an ultimatum and demanded he start going to a Christian therapist for his pornography addiction or else I was leaving him. His initial reaction was shock and unbelief that I'd give him such an ultimatum, so he lashed back by refusing to go. This made me more upset. I felt our marriage was worth nothing since Brad wouldn't even admit a problem or seek help to save our marriage. I was focusing all my energy and anger on Brad and not looking at any of my own issues.

Every turn my marriage took for the worse, I kept Aaron informed and depended on him for emotional support. He encouraged me and assured me I deserved better and he would be that better man for me. I took his every word to heart and leaned on him to pull me through the upcoming divorce I had planned. I kept telling myself that Aaron was a pastor and a man of God whom I could trust. I was putting him on a pedestal where he didn't belong and allowing him to manipulate me without recognizing what was happening.

Thoughts Become Reality

Brad became my enemy, standing in the way of my future dreams. I wanted Brad out of the picture as soon as possible. Arguments between us were becoming more frequent and intense. I told him I wanted a divorce and made him move into our basement. He wasn't in agreement with a divorce and thought my actions proved I was crazy and out of control. Steadfast in my decision, I hired a divorce attorney and proceeded with fees and paperwork to make it a reality.

Brad was given no choice but to also hire an attorney for protection and legal advice. We put our gorgeous home on the market and started looking for apartments to prepare for our separation. I accused Brad of being emotionally uninvolved and abusive to me for years. I threatened him with custody battles and said unthinkable words to hurt him without regret or regard for his feelings. I was far out of touch with God and only thinking about myself. I had a rude and defensive attitude. It was a nightmare, but a real one I couldn't wake up from.

Our home sold quickly. We legally separated and moved to our own apartment complexes. I was granted custody of the children during the week days and Brad had them on the weekends.

Please hear my heart on this. The honest truth is that this whole situation was a heart breaking time of turmoil and grief for us all. This was an extremely horrible time for our family and looking back on it breaks my heart to pieces. Its tragic effects were felt by every one of us, especially the children who were in my care as I attached myself to Aaron.

While thriving on my relationship with Aaron I was too blind and deceived to see he was using me as a replacement for his wife and a mother to his children. I spent an extensive amount of time at his home which consisted of cleaning his house, picking his kids up from school, taking his kids shopping, and providing daily needs he was unable to afford. I babysat his children, bought him many household things, and sat next to him smiling while he joked to his friends, I was his nanny. While out in public he lied about our relationship and hurt me emotionally with his words and actions. He was cautious to protect his reputation in the community. I accepted all of it for the small return of his assuring words that he would take care of me and he loved me.

Our relationship went on for months. I shudder to tell you that we eventually became physically involved in adultery. To protect himself as a pastor and in view of his own divorce hearings to come, Aaron made me promise that no matter what happened, I'd never tell a single soul about our affair. I agreed to his request while living in the darkness of my despair. I was in constant conflict and confused; falling deeper into the dark hole where I was living. I was anxious, scared, and feeling empty inside.

Brad and I were separated for a total of nine months. During this time we spent thousands of dollars in attorney's fees. I called Brad almost every single day for one reason or another, not realizing the reason was my heart was still clinging on to his. I felt guilt, shame, and grief for the pain I was causing him. My pain was excruciating and I felt torn apart! While we were separated, my life was no better for me than before; actually things were worse. My job became extremely difficult as a nurse. It was hard for me to focus as I fought with exhausting emotions. I lacked energy and strength and stopped exercising, while eating little and losing weight. My children were affected as seen in a pattern of their new negative behavior. I was experiencing migraine headaches although I never had headaches before. I even landed in the emergency room with excruciating pain forcing doctors to perform a cat scan of my head and thinking I possibly had an aneurysm.

The clock was ticking on the final divorce papers, and I was running out of time and options. But God was working on the scene. I started contemplating my actions, listening to my heart and convictions, wondering what I was doing to myself and my whole family. What did my future look like and what kind of life were my kids and I going to live when all was said and done? How would I provide for myself and the kids while being a full-time working, single mother? What was I doing to Brad and how could I hurt him so deeply like this? Things I once saw as liberating and better, I was seeing with a clearer and more logical vision. God was shining His light and truth on the situation and drawing me back to Him. And He waited patiently for my return.

Let me share some important information. I give God glory and Brad respect and honor for his efforts and the change of his heart. Even before we sold our home and legally separated, Brad begged me to stay with him. He eventually promised he would go to counseling and make things work out between us. He told me how sorry he was for everything and that God had shown him truths and his heart was changed. He vowed to be a better husband and father and love us like he had never done before. He wrote me an intimate letter of love and apology that I tore up and chose to disregard while hurling hate and rejection at him. I was convinced it was too late for us, and I was done. I wanted nothing to do with him and didn't want to believe him. Always lurking in the background was a destructive thing standing in the way of our marriage: Aaron.

Bizarre Happenings

"And have you forgotten the encouraging words God spoke to you as his children? He said, 'My child, don't make light of the Lord's discipline, and don't give up when he corrects you. For the Lord disciplines those he loves, and he punishes each one he accepts as his child.' As you endure this divine discipline, remember that God is treating you as his own children. Who ever heard of a child who is never disciplined by its father?" (Hebrews 12:5-7)

God persisted in speaking to my heart through His word, His people and other creative ways, but I continued to ignore Him. Bizarre things happened to me during this time. I was assaulted in a pet store when a lady started an argument with me over a newly-opened check-out lane. She waited for me and rammed her cart into me several times by the store exit and violently threatened me. The police were summoned, and I pressed charges. The case went to court and the lady was found guilty. She was given twenty four hours of community service and put on probation.

Run Away Boat

My children and I were in our SUV ready to leave our apartment complex parking lot. While we were getting ready to back out of the parking space I turned back and saw a boat coming at us at a fast speed. Did I say boat? Yes, a boat got loose from a hitch and was rolling right toward us. I was given seconds to throw the SUV into reverse and move just in the nick of time. The boat ran up on the sidewalk and damaged the area in front of where we were parked. We were blessed by the grace of God and not injured by such a freak accident.

Angry Shopper

While driving in a Target store parking lot, I was almost assaulted. A man became outraged as I drove next to him because he found it rude that in my impatience, I wouldn't stop to let him cross the street. As I drove past him, he started hitting my window and hurling nasty names at me. His daughter called me a stupid whore. I never would have thought about being called a whore before, except that it was extremely derogatory. But my current behavior with Aaron wasn't far from me acting like one, so I was feeling totally condemned and angry.

When I stopped my vehicle, the man randomly screamed and threatened me. With my pepper spray in hand, I cracked my window and threatened to spray him while talking with the dispatcher on the 911 phone line. She instructed me to remain calm and wait for the police who were on their way. The man was reprimanded by the police and no charges were filed.

Living out of God's will and out from under the umbrella of his protection is a dangerous place to venture. I was in that place, and I never want to go back.

Ready to Obey

It took time, but I finally started listening to God, hearing, and accepting what he was saying to me. He wanted me to stop end my affair with Aaron and make my marriage work with my husband. God gave me two important words to begin with: sever my relationship with Aaron and restore my relationship with my husband.

Constantly, I questioned God in this matter. I cried more tears than I thought I could produce. I hurt so badly, I didn't care if I were to die. Death would have been a relief from the agonizing pain I was going through. I just wanted it all to go away. I wanted to wake up one morning and find out it was all a dream. I wanted to go back and change all my bad and wrong choices. I wanted released from the horrific nightmare I was living.

Little by little and one day at a time I began obeying God. I called Brad and told him I wanted to try to make our marriage work. At that point, I didn't even know if Brad would take me back, but surprisingly his answer was yes. The hardest part was letting go of the powerful hold Aaron had on me and telling him my decision to go back to my husband. Aaron made it extremely difficult for me. He poured his heart out, and gave me lots of reasons I shouldn't do it. Then he piled on the guilt. He told me he would be the lonely boy looking through the window, watching Brad and me together while he was sad.

There were many challenging days I pushed through. I followed through with what I believed God wanted me to do. One crucial thing God told me was extraordinarily heart awakening and life changing. He told me, if I didn't go back to my husband and try to work things out, I'd die. This wasn't in an out loud verbal voice, but this revelation was spoken to my heart. It was frightening but compassionate at the same time. I realized later, God wasn't talking about a physical death but rather a spiritual one.

Brad and I were still separated but not divorced. I left my apartment and moved in with him in his larger apartment. It was a terribly complicated time as we made changes in ourselves and in our marriage. At first I lied and tried to hide the fact that Aaron and I had any physical relations together. I believed if Brad knew the truth, it would damage any chances of us restoring our marriage. Our first six weeks together were difficult and we had our doubts, but we made it though. We fought often, cried together, played the blame game, and started marriage counseling. The guilt from my affair kept me in bondage and gloom, knowing I was living a lie. That huge elephant was there! I knew I couldn't live with the guilt for the rest of my life. I made the decision to come clean to Brad and to everyone.

Adamant about my decision to tell the truth, I called Aaron and let him know I was going to tell Brad. He begged me not to tell Brad or anyone else. He reprimanded me and reminded me of the promise I made him. I'm so thankful I didn't let him manipulate me. I stood up to him. He was devastated and said any future chances of him becoming a pastor again would never happen. I felt no remorse for him because I knew he also needed to be accountable for his actions.

I was prepared to live with any consequences for my behavior. I rehearsed over again what and how I'd tell Brad. However, what I couldn't bring myself to do was tell him in person. I called him at work one afternoon and shared the whole truth about my affair over the phone. To say he was shocked would be making light of his response. He was appalled and devastated. He said it had crossed his mind but he wanted to believe the best. We didn't discuss the situation in detail over the phone; he wanted us to wait until he got home that evening to discuss it further. Because of the pain, the tears he choked back, and the disappointment I heard in my husband's voice, I started packing my things and thinking of where I'd go. I was ready for the battle when he got home. Quite frankly, I was so drained, emotionally exhausted, and frustrated; I couldn't defend myself in another fight. I was in the wrong, and I knew I deserved punishment.

Brad came home that evening with tears in his eyes and a mixture of emotions. His voice was shaky and his words were few. I let him know I was ready to leave and how sorry I was for everything. He looked at me as if I were stupid and told me he didn't want me to leave. Brad had spent time with God in prayer and made a decision to work out our marriage despite all that happened and what I had done. Secretly, I wanted Brad to yell at me, call me names, maybe hit me, or at least kick me to the curb. Any of those things would have helped with the guilt I was feeling. Instead, he loved me anyway and showed me forgiveness, mercy, and grace.

Had the tables been turned, I'm not sure I would have been strong enough to make the same decision. I don't know how hard it was for my husband or the battle he fought within himself. What I do know is it was harder to accept forgiveness than it would have been to endure rejection. After all, I deserved punishment, but did nothing to acquire forgiveness. Brad obeyed God and acted as a courageous and wonderful man after God's own heart. What an incredible testimony of God's love working in and through him. Thank you God.

28
Time of Restoration

Our hearts were incredibly happy to have our family back again. Brad and I were ready and willing to embark on our new journey together. We committed ourselves to God and each other. We were willing to do whatever it took to make things work. An amazing marriage counselor from our church met with us weekly to tackle our messes and teach us to do marriage God's way. The first thing we discussed was our individual problems and those desperately needed addressed before we could go to a deeper level. We worked on our faults we had denied in pride, and exposed our weaknesses. We were able to admit and openly accept each other just the way we were. We were completely broken.

What is of upmost importance is that we faced the challenges, accepted truths, and realized our ways didn't work. We opened our hearts and lives up to God and let him do new things in us and our marriage. "Therefore, if anyone is in Christ, the new creation has come: The old has gone, the new is here!" (2 Corinthians 5:17 NIV)

After an emotional or a physical affair, the recovery and restoration process is complicated. There are so many feelings involved and time becomes of essence for healing and the mending of hearts. My mind was still invaded by doubts proclaiming, "It's too late" and "it's never going to work." It was exceptionally hard to dismiss some of my negative thinking.

Our first assignment from our counselor was to start dating each other again. We set time apart to go to dinners, the movies and just to sit and talk over cups of coffee. We started to experience our relationship and discover one another in healthier ways. On New Year's Eve of 2005, our kids stayed with their grandparents for a weekend while Brad and I went to a retreat. This was a meaningful and eventful time for us as we engaged in deeper avenues of closeness.

On this particular retreat I had a real and miraculous experience. One night while I was asleep, I had a profound and vivid dream. In my dream God showed me what my life would be like if I divorced Brad and how empty I'd be and feel. It was similar to a clip from the movie The Christmas Carol. The dream was awful, and I experienced feelings of loneliness, despair, and chaos. I woke up from my dream shaking in the middle of the night and sat right up. When I looked ahead, Jesus was standing at the end of our bed. I wasn't still dreaming. This was real. Jesus didn't speak to me in an audible voice, but his peaceful presence made my dreadful feelings fade. It was quite an amazing experience. I received that message from Jesus loud and clear as I lay in disbelief of what I knew would happen if I went down the wrong path. It was simply a choice I needed to make: God's way or my way. I decided for sure that I wanted to choose God and act in obedience to Him, so I stayed with Brad. I'm thankful for the mercy and grace He gave me.

Restoring our marriage took patience, determination, time, and counseling. We are extremely grateful for everyone who stood by us and believed in us. We renewed our vows in the summer of 2006 with three inspiring couples including my best friend who did more than just stand by our side. They all gave us support, strength, and wisdom. They encouraged us to do God's will. It was a miraculous event in our lives, and we give God all the glory for what He has done in us and for us. We not only believe in miracles but we know our restored marriage is a miracle.

Positive Change

Today, my husband and I are doing just great! We have a true, deep, and meaningful marriage that has been a reward for all of our hard work and God's saving grace. God has blessed us in more ways than

I can count or tell you. We handle problems and life altogether differently and make sure we keep God in the center of our hearts and our marriage. Yes, we still have our moments and some bad days. We still have fights and disagreements and say things we shouldn't. Nothing is perfect. If we expect perfection, then our expectations are too high.

I'm deeply in love with the man of God I've been given. Brad treats me exceptionally well; his love for me is evident in his words and actions. He does so much for me and works hard to provide for our family. Brad grocery shops, cooks, acts as our handyman, and is caring and supportive. He has willingly and gladly been delivered from the pornography addiction. He is there when I need him, and I just can't say enough about how wonderful things in our lives have become.

I've learned to respond to God with submission and obedience. I've learned that God will always lead us in the right direction and down the appropriate path when we seek him. It's not easy. I don't always want to do it. I don't always make the right choices and decisions, but I do my best to trust God and follow Him and His ways. "Seek the Kingdom of God above all else, and live righteously, and he will give you everything you need." (Matthew 6:33)

God sees the beginning from the end. He knows what is best and when we try to do things our way, it does not work well or work for long. Our lives have purpose, and we have a creator who is more concerned with what He can do in us, than what He can do for us. "The Lord is like a father to his children, tender and compassionate to those who fear him. For he knows how weak we are; he remembers we are only dust." (Psalm 103: 13-14)

Home Is Where the Heart Is

We were desperate for a fresh start and thought it best to move away from the scenery holding bad memories. Brad tried for months to land a job in South Carolina, so we made a visit to explore the area. It's so pretty, has great beaches, and the weather is grand. But as hard as we prayed and tried in our own strength, nothing happened. I mean nothing. It took us some time, but we finally realized once again, God had a different plan.

Brad started looking for a house in our current area so we could get out of the apartment. The timing was ideal when he found a home close to his work, and it had just decreased in price. We had some great friends who were realtors who stepped in right away to help. We visited the home and immediately fell in love with it. It was large, beautiful colonial home which included a sun room, walk-out basement, and more than we had before in our previous home. The main dilemma and concern was the cost. We weren't confident we could get a loan for the price. We prayed and prayed. We surrendered the situation to God and we decided we didn't even want the house if it wasn't His plan and best for us.

Paperwork was filed, and the waiting began. A few days passed when the phone call finally came with the loan approval. In total amazement to all of us it was almost exactly the price of the home! We jumped up and down with excitement and hugged each other in joy! We were so thankful for another miracle. We moved in our new gorgeous home in 2006 and have been appreciative and enjoying it every single day since. With God all things are possible! This I truly know and believe. (Matthew 19:26)

Marriage Requires Team-Work

We have learned a lot about our relationship. We continue to learn and grow daily. Marriage requires time, energy, communication, and sacrifice. It's easy in the beginning of new relationships to dismiss faults and annoyances in the other person. We naturally take a profound interest in them and see them through "rose colored glasses."

As time goes on, infatuation fades and we begin to see the other person differently, possibly becoming frustrated by little things we let go before. This is normal. Just know and remember this: no matter what phase we are in of our marriage, marriage always takes work.

The key to success in marriage (as I have learned) is this: Work to improve you and never try to change the other person. We don't have control over other people. We can only control ourselves. Sacrifice, submission, devotion to God, and putting God first is most important to keeping a marriage together. Without God at the center of a marriage, it won't work well or be truly blessed. Love is an amazing thing. God is Love! Every day is an opportunity to work at our marriages so we can keep them happy and thriving. "Dear friends, let us continue to love one another, for love comes from God. Anyone who loves is a child of God and knows God. But anyone who does not love does not know God, for God is love." (1 John 4:7-8)

Relationships are one of the most beautiful and encouraging gifts. We were made to journey together. Unfortunately, the enemy of your soul will attack after you position yourself in an intimate and vulnerable setting. When you share personal details with others to be helpful or encouraging, you may doubt, have fear, and feel anxious, wondering if you hurt someone's feelings or offended someone. You may feel shame and believe you were too forthcoming, rude, and obnoxious, or that maybe you shared too much.

The thoughts go on, and the fear discourages. But remember, "God causes everything to work together for the good of those who love God and are called according to his purpose for them." (Romans 8:28) Even if we did say something wrong or offensive, God can fix it and soften people's hearts to understand us and where we are coming from. We are an imperfect people coming together loving God and loving each other. If the devil can break us apart, we have no friendships or support. Divorce can result and families divide. Therefore, we have to stand strong against the ploys of the enemy and know that "God is for us and not against us." (Romans 8:31) And Jesus says," the gates of hell shall not prevail against the Church!" (Matthew 16:18)

We are the Church, built upon the rock. Let's take off the masks, crash down the walls, and enjoy real and sincere relationships without fear. "Don't just pretend to love others. Really love them. Hate what is wrong. Hold tightly to what is good. Love each other with genuine affection, and take delight in honoring each other." (Romans 12:9-10)

Be real. Be Fearless.

29
Revelations Bring Healing

I walked around in life with a deep yearning in my inner self for love and approval. It took me years to discover who I ultimately wanted and needed this love from was my father. I was neglected by him, emotionally mistreated, and never given a chance to know the true love of a dad.

Ever since we started communicating again after the birth of my son, our relationship was shallow and on edge. My dad kept himself at a distance and managed to make excuses why he couldn't take time to visit. Interestingly enough, he made frequent visits to my brother in New Mexico, innumerable hunting trips around the country, and took his step grandchildren to Disney World. He went on vacations and found the time to indulge in his own likings but gave me empty excuses for not spending time with me and my family. Jealousy raged in my heart, my stomach churned with nausea, and rejection flowed through my veins as tears streamed freely. I was given no choice but to accept the circumstances. I walked around feeling hurt and not good enough for him.

In ten years he managed to visit me only three times. The drive between us was seven hours. We made visits to him by taking our kids to see family in the summers or on holidays. When we did venture to his neck of the woods, we were always greatly disappointed. Even after our long trip, we were not a priority to him. If someone else was in town, that person came first. If other plans arose for him, he would change ours. My dad would expect us to work around his schedule. And after we were in town for days, he'd manage to meet us for dinner for only a couple hours.

Most of our communication was by phone or email. Phone conversations were unpleasant. He always managed to thrive on tangents and think it funny to taunt me relentlessly. He told me course jokes, made fun of my Christianity, and loved to say how spoiled my kids were. Email conversations were even worse, because he wrote many mean and outright nasty comments that were ridiculous. He emailed me nasty sexual jokes. This man would speak to me like no dad should ever speak to his daughter. He was inappropriate.

I prayed for him and hoped for a sincere change in his heart. When I told him I was praying for him or spoke about God, he mocked me and threw my previous sins in my face. He harassed me and called me stupid for tithing at church, asking when the church would in turn ever help me. He made comments on Facebook to demean and condemn me for any inspirational posts I wrote and publically humiliated me. For my birthdays he never sent a card and rarely called. I tried hard and did all I knew how, to have a healthy, productive relationship with my dad. I accepted him for who he was, rationalized his behavior, and forgave him often. I came to a place in my heart with God's strength when I was able to ignore his rude and outrageous comments. Either I wouldn't respond, or if I did, I'd respond in love. He wasn't appreciative of my kindness and mocked me more saying I was patronizing him.

A few years ago, I hit rock bottom in my relationship with my dad. He sent me a vicious email that tore my heart apart. His mockery towards me for being a Christian was unbearable and disturbing. He hurt me deeply by disrespecting my mom also, saying we were both crazy and needed to be seeing a psychiatrist. He lashed out, called me names, and continued to manipulate me. I read one of his hurtful emails in disbelief several times over, trying to understand him, but each time I cried more. I was unable to carry the burden any further of feeling responsible to maintain a relationship with him. I responded to his email after time and prayer.

I told him I'd no longer endure the stress, anxiety, or pain he caused me. I wouldn't let him speak to me the way he had. I spoke my mind and told him I felt he was never a real father to me. I poured my heart out to him and ended our relationship. I made him aware I'd continue to pray for him, and if he wanted to contact me, he knew where I lived. I blocked him on Facebook and blocked his email address. I placed boundaries to protect myself and my family from him.

It was the first time ever I felt peace from God to sever my relationship with my dad. During the months after, God revealed amazing discoveries in the midst of terrible pain. God gave me revelations which were eye opening and helpful for the healing of my heart. I became aware of some truths about my dad's hardened heart. I knew he was deceived and unable to love because he didn't know love. I had tolerated abuse and pain without setting boundaries in a desperate attempt to make him approve of me. Sadly, I never got what I needed from the one I wanted it from the most. Thankfully, I've been set free from the bondage of approval addiction. I know I'm approved of and loved by God. God is the only one we need approval and acceptance from.

When I think about my dad, I envision him just where I left him. I decided to bury him mentally. He lies dead in a shiny smooth black casket accented by silver handles and a soft inner lining of white cloth. He wears a black suit with a white button-down dress shirt, his tie is red with silver vertical lines, and a red carnation sticks out of his left chest pocket. His short, gray hair is neatly groomed, and the color matches his mustache. His glasses are straight on his face. Seeing him in that place where he lies breathless, I realize he can't hurt me anymore. I finally feel safe, able to taste the sweetness of triumph, but its bitter sweet.

In my imagination, my dad Karl died in the summer of 2010 from chronic heart failure. He left behind a daughter who truly loved him more than he knew, because he never took a chance to know her heart or love her back. He left behind two wonderful grandchildren that are his own flesh and blood. The ones he never sacrificed time, energy, or maturity for. Karl fought a long, stubborn, and heartbreaking fight with "heart disease." It was extremely painful to watch him make choices and decisions that were selfish and made reconciliation with him impossible. There weren't many who attended his funeral, probably due to a lack of respect for a man who lived too much for himself. I said good-bye to him without shedding a tear. My lack of tears wasn't a response from a cold heart, but rather a justified response from being numb and feeling void of any compassion for a man who only hurt, rejected, and abandoned me time and again. My tears for him were used up; they fell when he called me names, cut me deeply with snide remarks, and wounded me with disrespect and condescension.

He left me with gaping wounds without an apology or assuming any responsibility for his behavior. How can such a man with the name of "Dad" have been so cold and demeaning? I don't try to understand him anymore, I accept the fact he is no longer part of my life and that he was the one who missed out. I don't say this with arrogance; I say this because I've learned from Jesus that my worth is much more than what I was shown by my dad.

I still pray for him and I hope one day he will have a "heart transplant" and become a new person in Christ. Sometimes I dream my doorbell rings, and he is standing there wanting to reconcile. I forgive him for all he has done and by doing this I not only set him free, but I'm set free, too.

If he ever gets his hands on this book I want him to know, I'm still praying for him. It is possible he may read this book one day, because I am the one who buried him; he is only dead to me.

Mom

My mother and I have a mended relationship that allows us to accept each other as we are. Libby lives in New Mexico with her fourth husband. My family and I endured multiple visits with her over the years. The visits weren't always pleasant. She acted out irrationally by yelling about silly situations and fighting with her husband. She presented with paranoid behavior and even scratched her husband, making him bleed on a trip while we were all in a mini-van together. My kids are frightened and uncomfortable around her. We tolerate and do our best to enjoy her company. She possesses moments of clarity and reason, but it doesn't outweigh her crazy behavior.

Reluctantly, she has shared with me her shattered dreams, disappointments, and daunting past. Libby wasn't proven to be loved as a child; she experienced neglect from her father, and her mother was an alcoholic who died in her early 50's. She was abandoned from her own family and abused by ex-husbands.

I don't believe my mom raised me the best she could. Even in her darkest of circumstances, she always had the choice to love and protect me, as well as the choice to run and get help. Her decisions were selfish, leaving us kids in continuous neglect and harm. I have, however, forgiven her. I choose to love her anyway, because she is my mom. This doesn't take away my pain or make her actions right. Forgiveness releases me from anger and bitterness towards her; forgiveness allows God to fill me with compassion and His supernatural power to love her anyway.

I've flat out told her she was a bad mom. I recently asked her why she didn't protect and care for me like a mom should. She insists that she did the best she could. She believes she wasn't a bad mom. I tried to reason with her and go into depth of why she needs to take responsibility and stop playing the victim card. She insists she has blocked out some of her memories. Libby is not able to be reasoned with, and her perspective is screwed up. Recently she dared ask me, "What was so bad about your childhood?" It was at that instant in time I realized she is mentally unstable and unable to be reasoned with. Her reality and mental health is distorted. You can't reason with her. I have tried.

My mom's past life was one of deep sorrow and pain. On several occasions her abusive second husband threatened to kill her. Today she holds a full-time job as a preschool teacher and loves the little ones she cares for. Her life has some stability, and I give her credit for how far she has come, considering where she once was. She knows of Jesus, but does not have a personal relationship or walk with Him. I love my mom and pray that God will use me to add value and meaning in her life.

30
A Perfectionist's Confession

*I*t's presumptuous to look at someone else and think their life is easy. Never assume someone just woke up one day and had a magic wand waved over them to take away all their problems. Never compare yourself with people and envy what they have or who they are. We don't know and we may never understand their trials, pain, and the circumstances they are going through or have gone through before. People only tell and share what they want us to know. Some have worked hard to get where they are.

Life is not easy! It's a journey of taking one step at a time, growing in our faith, working through problems, and trusting Jesus in all things. Life is challenging and requires depending on God to see us through. If it weren't for Jesus who snatched me from the enemy's hand long ago, I wouldn't be here today! I thank God for who He is and all He has done in my life. Let us all go forth today and everyday loving God more and also sharing that same love with others. "We love each other because he loved us first." (1 John 4:19)

Allow me to get real with you, since truth is refreshing, and vulnerability knocks down barriers, drawing people closer. I have a secret to share with you: I live my life as a perfectionist.

As a perfectionist, I am not at all perfect. I live every day trying to bite my tongue and remember who I am in Christ. I constantly fight the urge to be my old self while surrendering my old habits to God so I can walk as the new creation Jesus made me to be. "This means that anyone who belongs to Christ has become a new person. The old life is gone; a new life has begun!" (2 Corinthians 5:17) NIV

It's hard to accept, but the truth is that my past does define part of who I am. It doesn't matter if I like it or not, it's a fact. I may have been raised and defined by strangers, but I've been transformed by the supernatural power of God! I choose to take the good with the bad and trust God to renew my mind and change me daily into who He wants me to be. I'm often hard on myself and impatient while I try to make changes to better my character, thoughts, and choices. Thankfully, God knows my heart, intentions, and motives, and He gently reels me back into Him, reminding me that I am a work in progress. I have to submit and surrender myself to God often as I try to do life in my own strength. I've learned that apart from God I can do nothing. "I am the vine; you are the branches. If you remain in me and I in you, you will bear much fruit; apart from me you can do nothing." (John 15:5 NIV)

Every day I live with worries and try my best to entrust them to God in prayer, while at times I contradict my faith and waver in doubt. I am a wife, mother, nurse, writer, and friend. I carry those responsibilities and more I can't bear on my own. Many days I try to do everything in my own strength, and I hit my pillow at night having made mistakes and wondering if I failed.

As a perfectionist I hate making a mistake, let alone admitting to one. And trust me—I make mistakes on a daily basis. Thankfully, God in his mercy reminds me that making mistakes is an opportunity for humility. And mistakes prove I am only human.

What keeps me from failing is Jesus Christ! He is my strength in my weakness. His mercy is new every morning. When I read His word and pray He strengthens me with power I can't explain, it is heavenly and comes from His awesomeness. He fills me with love and the fruit of the Spirit to carry on and live His ways. He encourages me to keep on keeping on and to trust in Him no matter how things look or how I feel. Jesus reminds me to never give up and put all my hope in Him.

Perfectionism will never work to give us the peace and security we desire. The only thing that offers what we need is a perfect God. "God's way is perfect. All the LORD's promises prove true. He is a shield for all who look to him for protection." (2 Samuel 22:31)

How do you see yourself? Do you see yourself as the world sees you, or do you see yourself as God does? People in this world will focus on your faults, your flaws, and your weaknesses. They will tell you that you aren't good enough, not capable, not educated enough, not strong enough, and you just don't measure up. God looks at your strengths, your inner beauty, your heart, your potential, your accomplishments, and most importantly when He looks at you, He sees Himself in you! He sees your future.

When you look at yourself, know you are a work in progress created in Christ's image. God loves you, He has His hand upon you, and He is doing great things for you and in you. Take the expectations off yourself to be perfect and understand you will never meet them. Place your focus and trust in Jesus Christ. He will never fail you!

Longing for Grace

Because of my childhood, I vowed to do a better job parenting my children than my parents did with me. I do my best to teach my children right from wrong. They have been raised in a Christian home, gone to church, and personally witnessed the difference of being in or out of God's will. I pray for them, encourage them, and instruct them to seek God in all they do. With all this being said and done, I will admit I live with unreachable expectations for my children to be "Christ-like Super Stars."

Sometimes, the reality of life reveals disheartening choices and decisions my children have made. During these times, I ask myself, "Where did I go wrong?" Suddenly, this morning, it hit me. Truth Himself spoke to my heart and said, "Does not our Father in Heaven ask Himself and wonder the same thing?" God has taught us well, given us instructions, given human examples, laid out the consequences of sin for us, and even handed us instructions in a manual for daily living called the Bible. Think of the cross: at the cost of his one and only son, God gave us a blameless, living sacrifice.

Even still, we cave to sin. We give in. We listen to our own wisdom, we listen to others, we believe lies, and our flesh battles the spirit. Good vs. Evil will be a constant fight for every one of us until our death.

What is the answer and what do we do? Awake, oh soul, awake, rise up and fight! Recognize the inner struggle. Expose the enemy and the lies exactly for what they are. Then lay it all at the cross, at the feet of Jesus. Repent, surrender, submit, obey, and accept with a grateful heart our "redo."

Today is a new day; a new day to live in and walk in the strength and power of Jesus. Will you allow your heart to visit the cross today? Allow Jesus to embrace you and dust you off. Hear Him say, "Your sins are forgiven, now go and sin no more." (Luke 7:48)

Freedom is here! Oh taste and see that the Lord is good. "Therefore, since we are surrounded by such a great cloud of witnesses, let us throw off everything that hinders and the sin that so easily entangles, and let us run with perseverance the race marked out for us." (Hebrews 12:1 NIV)

When we look at our children and wonder what happened, remember to offer them the same grace and mercy our heavenly Father offers us. We are all children of God. Grace and mercy are gifts we can't afford to refuse and gifts we need to offer freely.

A Mother's Secret

Some have said children are brutally honest and I can certainly attest to that. It isn't the offensiveness from the honesty that's hard to swallow, but the responsibility of the truth we have to accept.

Without bragging I feel confident in saying I am a great mother. I do my best to parent my children in an honorable, sacrificial, and loving way. They have things I never dreamed of when I was their age. They have love, support, grace, discipline, and a well-rounded childhood. I have protected them from harm, stood up for them, provided their needs, and gone out of my way to be the mother for them I never had. Do I offer or give perfection? No. I will be the first to admit and accept the mistakes I've made with my children.

This brings me to disclose a hard struggle I've battled with since the age of thirteen: an eating disorder. My eating disorder was my secret. My secret was only supposed to affect me and no one else. It was my body and I could treat it as I wanted. No one could tell me what to do with food or without it. No one could judge me for how I felt and what I did with my feelings. I wouldn't even allow getting pregnant at the age of twenty affect my secret. I was well aware that raising children when I had an eating disorder put them at higher risk for developing an eating disorder. This fact only pushed me harder to hide my secret.

Around my children I tried not to talk about how fat I felt or how fat I thought I looked. I tried to eat normally and not make my eating habits look strange. I tried to work out normally and not let my kids see my obsession. I tried these things for years, and it was working. But I was living in deception.

In due time, it became exclusively apparent to me that my secret was never hidden. It was always revealing itself through my actions and words. During time in therapy I was "clued in" by my therapist that my thirteen year old daughter was exhibiting some eating disorder habits of her own. My response was denial. How could this be true? How come I didn't see it? I kept a close watch on her for any signs.

Let's discuss a hard lesson learned here; I didn't see the signs of her eating disorder because the signs she possessed weren't anything other to me than normal behavior. Ironically, her abnormal behavior was something we shared. Reality hit me hard, and I realized I needed acceptance and healing. I had to get better so my daughter would get better. I had to mirror normal eating and correct body image behavior so she would recognize and know what was right. It was a time of sacrifice and becoming aware of how I was affecting myself and my own daughter.

You know that moment when your hand is caught in the cookie jar, and it's impossible to lie? That was me one evening when I was confronted by my own child. My daughter and I were in my bedroom looking through a scrapbook of some old childhood photos of me. She looked at a photo of when I was eight years old, pointed at it, and asked, "Do you think you are fat here?" I replied, "No." She turned the pages and pointed to a ten year old photo of me and asked, "Do you think you are fat here?" My reply was again, "No." Her third question as she looked right at me was, "Do you think you are fat now?" I replied, "No."

Concerned and suspecting she felt fat herself, I assured her it was normal to think she was fat but told her she was beautiful and perfect. She immediately turned the arrow in the right direction and pointed it at me. She said, "I know about your eating disorder." My stomach flipped, my head was boggled, and my spirit sank within. What was she talking about? How could she know my secret? So I asked naively, "What are you talking about?" She proceeded to explain she overheard me on the phone with a friend talking about my bulimia and she admitted to knowing things from the past. She had wanted to tell me, but my attitude wasn't approachable. Here in this moment, I was the child, and she was the parent. If you have ever been in this position you know as well as I do, it is a place of "rock bottom," and it's humiliating.

I had a heart-to-heart talk with my daughter and explained I was in therapy and getting better. I promised her I wouldn't make myself throw up anymore. She looked at me with her tender, sweet, young eyes filled with concern and worry as I comforted and assured her all was well. I put on my "Mommy Pants" and declared to myself I wasn't about to be a mom who puts her children in distress and remains selfish.

This was a defining moment in my life; the moment where I learned a lot about myself, my daughter and about parenting. I've made some huge progress since this time in my recovery from an eating disorder. I'm not only doing this for myself, but for my family. My heart is extremely blessed as I've seen improvement and changes in my daughter as well. She is not calling herself fat anymore, binging, and restricting or mimicking my abnormal behavior. We are together on a path of a healthy, happy, and a rightly motivated relationship with food and each other.

31
To Binge or not to Binge

*H*aving weaknesses and sharing our personal struggles can make us feel uneasy, insecure, and on guard to people's thoughts or comments. None of us likes to be judged or looked at differently. However, I find vulnerability necessary to being truthful in helping myself and others discover freedom.

There has been pain and many issues I've faced in life, but this one in particular has been the most challenging. I don't share my wounds and this deep matter because I'm seeking sympathy. I'm well aware of the choices and decisions I made and how consequences find me out. I'm not prideful either, where I'd lie and push this aside without admitting my problem. My hopes and intentions for telling these things are to help set captives free. The fact is, truth equals freedom, and knowing we are not alone helps set our minds at ease and shed light on our dark, hidden secrets. It's my goal to help you by letting you know, you are not alone.

The diagnosis revealed to me by my therapist was "Non Specified Eating Disorder." I was rather surprised because I always called myself a "controlled bulimic." It is ironic this was the name I chose for my eating disorder since there is no control whatsoever involved with bulimia.

My eating disorder began in my early childhood. Raging negative emotions filled my heart and mind daily as I lived in constant stress and harm's way. I was surrounded by the enemy, laid out in the middle of a battle I was defenseless to fight. With no way to understand my circumstances and no route of escape, food became my peace, comfort and my best friend. I ate candy, cookies, pie, cake, ice cream, and whatever I got my hands on. These foods allured me with their delightful smell and rich sweet taste creating an exhilarating sensation. When I ate these foods, I was instantly transported to a positive emotional state of mind where I experienced pleasure. Sugar was my main food group and the only negative feeling was my conscience and my stomach pain, but I chose to ignore them.

Knowledge is Power

Any addiction is tough to beat. It is almost impossible to conquer it solo, and it's challenging even with someone's help. Anything in our lives we spend too much time thinking about or involving ourselves with can be or become an addiction. Common addictions include alcohol, drugs, cigarettes, gambling, pornography, stealing, and working.

One common addiction less talked about because of shame or embarrassment; is gluttony, or food addiction. People over-indulge with food, in an effort to numb pain or create a positive mood diminishing negative feelings. A repercussion of binge eating or emotional eating is obesity. Obesity can also be caused by physical or emotional diseases, or medications. (Note: Not all people with food addictions are overweight.) The effects of food addictions can a toll on a person's body and cause chronic conditions such as diabetes, arthritis, chronic pain, heart disease, kidney disease, or high blood pressure.

Some people may have emotional disorders linked to their compulsion with food such as depression, anxiety, fear, or even suicidal ideations. There are many types of eating disorders. Help and healing is available, but we have to personally want to get well and surrender any excuses to make that happen.

Facing Demons

Some days I still struggle with food and a distorted body image. The battle is difficult as it seeks to devour my identity and consume my strength and time. I've never been underweight or endured a stay in rehab or a hospital for my eating disorder. While I've been to counseling and therapy I'm still in the process of breaking free and allowing God to heal me of this disease and psychological disorder. I'm not where I need to be, but I thank God I'm not where I used to be.

I will openly share with you some thoughts that are common for me and others with a distorted body image and eating disorders. "I am fat." "I am not good enough." "I have to lose weight." "I need to be thin to be popular, liked, accepted, or even loved." "If I am thin I will be happier." "If I can fit into these jeans my life will be perfect." For years I believed that if I was fat, I'd be worthless. My greatest fear in life was the fear of being fat. Being thin meant everything to me.

Both times I was pregnant, I used the opportunity to eat whatever and whenever I wanted. I assumed since I was pregnant, I couldn't be fat. I gained seventy pounds each time. And when I delivered my first child at the age of twenty, I weighed in at two hundred and fourteen pounds, standing five feet and four inches tall. During both pregnancies, I developed PIH (Pregnancy Induced Hypertension), my labor was induced because of a dangerously high blood pressure and toxin in my body. Had I taken care of myself, that condition may have been prevented, and I wouldn't have endangered my life or my babies.

Even though I'm fit now, the mirror lies to me. I don't see myself the way others do. I see a bulging stomach and feel disappointment because I look fat. I find it interesting that I can mentally gain ten pounds in one day because I see myself that much bigger in my reflection.

With the help of therapy I'm learning to make peace with my body and not be best friends with the scale. For years I'd weigh myself daily and be ashamed if the number wasn't perfect. How miserable I was to let a scale, a set of numbers, dictate how I thought and felt about myself.

What is a "perfect number" anyway? It was a number I had made up in my mind as a goal to obtain happiness. The perfect number always changed and constantly decreased even when I reached it. For a total of eleven years the scale reflected almost the same number, varying up or down only five pounds. I was still incapable of realizing or accepting, I wasn't fat. I was at a healthy weight my body was able to maintain.

Please hold this truth close to your heart: the scale simply tells us how much our bodies weigh; it does not dictate our value or worth as a person. Someone will always be better looking than you, thinner than you, richer than you, and smarter than you. When we stop comparing ourselves to others and fully enjoy who God created us to be, life becomes more pleasurable. We begin to like ourselves more. ~ Live life to the fullest and be yourself. God made you different, unique and you on purpose!

Resisting Temptation

Some choices we make can give us inner peace. I've learned if I say no to the brownies, then I don't spin viciously into a cycle of regret, guilt, binging, purging, and disappointment. I won't have to spend two hours on the treadmill to work off a generous bowl of chocolate cookie dough ice cream topped with chocolate syrup and whipped cream if I say no first. However, sometimes we give into those sweet temptations calling our names and overindulge. Then we feel like a failure. We are not a failure when this happens. And who said you can't have dessert anyway? If we make wrong choices we can learn from them instead of beating ourselves up over them. We can let go and realize we are a work in progress, not a design of perfection. God offers us hope, strength, and a life-long journey of spiritual growth. When we take our eyes off ourselves and our problems, we are able to better focus on God. Let us truly desire God and all He has to offer us. We can't go wrong with that decision.

32
Dare to Pray

Overwhelmed and exhausted is how I lived most of my days. I battled with negative emotions and feelings that tried to annihilate me. I was boxed in by fear, anxiety, worry, and stress. Living life in that box, I was too scared to step out.

As a prisoner, I was unable and too scared to jump out of my cell block. God spoke to my heart one day and showed me how I was allowing these four emotions to control me. He told me it was time to jump out of the box and experience the freedom he had ready and available. God told me that I should be more afraid to stay in the box than to get out of it. I tried time after time to jump out of the box. I'd get out, start to feel better, and life would seem good until a problem or difficult storm would come my way. During rough times, instead of running to God I'd run back into my box, hunker down, and live in a place of familiarity. It was a wrong response, but its human nature to return to our old ways. I continued in that same pattern for a couple of years until my box started crashing down on me. Worry only made me feel worse, and panic became my first response to any problem. Stress was making me physically ill. I became extremely desperate for change.

Courage to Change

Fatigued and distraught after a hard day at work, I decided it was time to go for a refreshing walk. On my walks, I spent time with God in prayer and shared my heart in anticipation of His response. Walking around my neighborhood on a cool and sunny fall day, I prayed an exuberant, meaningful, and life-changing prayer. I poured out my heart to God and told him I was unable to do life anymore the way I was doing it. I wasn't asking to die, but I told God that if I had to keep living the way I was living and in the same turmoil day after day, I'd rather not live anymore. Ready, willing, and open to God and whatever He had for me, I wanted a complete make-over to learn a new way of living the Christian life. Deep in my heart I knew there had to be some way to get out of the terrible rut of disaster my mind was in. I knew there was hope, and I was calling on His name.

Ready or Not

About a week after my passionate prayer asking God to change me, I sat down to journal. It was then God spoke to my heart and gave me this specific message:

I pray and ask God for help, for Him to rescue me from trials and various things in life that consume me. I pray and ask for anxiety and fear to be gone and for my stress and exhaustion to disappear. All along I hear Him asking me, "Are you ready?" "Yes Lord. Yes, I am ready," I reply.

Time goes on, and the same things happen over again with no changes! Until today. Now I get it! The question is, "Are you ready?" The word "ready" means: "completely prepared or in fit condition for immediate action or use."

How can I be ready if I am living in fear and not trusting God? How can I be ready if I believe the lies of the enemy instead of God's word? How can I be ready if I am trusting in and relying on myself and my own thoughts and plans instead of God's? How can I be ready if I think I am in control even though it is God who is? How can I be ready if I am not reading, meditating or speaking God's word? How can I be ready if I am not praying, being still, or spending time with God? How can I be ready if I am spending more time with my problem than with God?

So my answer should have been, "No, I am not ready." It is time to climb out of the pit one step at a time and make one change at a time. This takes discipline, obedience, time, faith, and trust in the

Lord. It is time to grow up and change my ways. There is work to do beyond myself. God will renew my mind, purify my heart, sanctify me, and transform me. He is ready, willing, and able. Am I ready? "Yes, Lord, Yes, I AM READY!"

God's answer to me through my writing was incredible, inspiring, and truthful. As hard as it was to swallow, I definitely knew it was time to grow up emotionally and spiritually. It was time to start living and moving into all the awesome promises of God. It was time for a change, and I was ready. That writing took place in October 2009. In no time as usual, the holidays came fast, and I found myself caught up in the 2009 Christmas Season.

Reflecting on the Season

Ready or not, every year the holiday's come. Each year no matter how hard I try or how I prepare, it stresses me out. I want to know, who put the stress in Christmas? It can take as much emotional energy as it does physical energy to create a "Merry Christmas." Let's get real here; Christmas stresses most of us out! We start with a budget, but we overspend. For some reason we need to buy everyone a gift, and we almost always end up forgetting someone or adding people to the list. We bake cookies or make goodies, but there are never enough left after we eat them all. Then we complain we gained ten pounds during the holiday season.

The tree needs to be decorated, but first we need a tree. The artificial tree is in the basement and supposed to make life easier, but this year we decide we need a real one. The real tree will cost eighty dollars, but it's worth the smell of fresh pine in the house. It was a grand idea until it becomes impossible to get it straight in the tree stand, and we find ourselves yelling at our family, "Is it straight now?" Once decorated and beautiful as can be, it eventually dries out, and we vacuum thousands of pine needles scattered all through the house. Now we are complaining because the pine needles are everywhere.

The outside of the house needs decorated but the lights can't be the same color as last year. The neighbors put up hundreds of lights, so we need more. It's time to decorate the inside of the house; it looks great until we see something new at the store we have to buy or see a friend who did a better job. The Christmas card list shouldn't be long because we can share photos online and use email. However, some people are "old fashioned" or not familiar with today's technology so we need to send cards and photos via the post office.

Family is important during the holiday season. The time comes to figure out whose turn it is to visit whom. No matter who travels or who hosts, there is still tension and anxiety when people are taken out of their ordinary routine and schedule. We need to prepare, clean, cook, and plan entertainment. There are some relatives we need to impress or "put up with" while we visit with them for this once a year occasion.

The dog needs groomed; travel arrangements need to be made. We have to sort through and decide what invitations we will accept or decline for the upcoming festivities. Shopping can be hectic whether done online or in the stores. All the presents will need wrapped and labeled. People will shop and buy clothes they only wear to one party. Then the clothes will sit in their closets until next year when that outfit is outdated and they need a new one.

Christmas morning will eventually come and we'll engage in new or traditional festivities. Gifts that took a long time to find and energy to wrap will be torn open in seconds. Some gifts will be perfect, while some will need the receipt and require a trip back to the store for a refund or exchange. Kids will cry because they didn't get what they asked for. Some families will fight and argue over stupid things that will bring havoc in a home and ruin any greatly anticipated memories. Turkeys will burn, and some won't cook. In most homes and families, the time, money, energy, and all the people put into making one special Christmas Day won't be what they expected it to be. But don't get discouraged and ban this coming Christmas yet. There is hope and a better way to do all of this. Let's challenge ourselves to dig into the deeper and more meaningful reasons for Christmas and live them out.

True Meaning

Christmas Day is when we choose to celebrate the birth of our Savior, Jesus Christ. Giving gifts on Christmas is a tradition based on the gifts that were given by the Magi to Jesus after His birth. These gifts were gold, frankincense, and myrrh. Sadly over time, Christmas has become commercialized and based on money rather than the joy of giving and creating cherished memories.

It's time to take a stand for what we believe, and put "Christ" back into Christmas. Sometimes we need to go "back to the basics." We can do that during the Christmas season by making choices which are realistic and simple. Let's give to others because we want to and because it will greatly bless them. Remember to make time for family and friends, create laughter, and enjoy your relationships. "Do not conform any longer to the pattern of this world, but be transformed by the renewing of your mind. Then you will be able to test and approve what God's will is--his good, pleasing and perfect will." (Romans 12:2 NIV)

Every one of our lives is significant. Every choice we make matters. Our thinking determines our perspective and our actions. The truth is sometimes we let the world's way rule our thinking and actions, and we end up allowing this to make us selfish. Let us take a look into our own hearts and ask God to reveal our motives. Let us allow God to renew our minds with His word, His wisdom, and His revelation, creating a paradigm in our thinking so we can live more in His ways!

Don't hold too tightly to your cash, it can slip away. Don't be too fond of all the things you possess; they can be repossessed. Don't be haughty, egotistical or arrogant; those mindsets and attitudes are an illusion created by this world to keep you in a place of pride. The things of this world that make a difference, the things that create happiness in hearts, things that last forever, and things to cherish are what we all carry inside. They are gifts given to us by God to share with one other: gifts of love, giving and sharing, lending a helping hand, praying for a hurting person or family, encouraging someone who's discouraged, and standing up for a good cause.

As we go into the next holiday season, let us search our hearts and not our wallets. Yes, we can do "good" in the form of giving and buying someone a gift. Yes, God blesses a cheerful giver. But don't make life about money or things. Make this season and your life about loving God and loving people. When we love, we make a difference of significance that will last forever.

33

Testing Faith

"For you know that when your faith is tested, your endurance has a chance to grow. So let it grow, for when your endurance is fully developed, you will be perfect and complete, needing nothing." (James 1:3-4)

This year it was our turn to host my in-laws and extended family for the holidays. While we were enjoying a nice meal at a restaurant, I was struck by a sudden onset of pain. The pain was odd and concerned me. It seemed to mimic the symptoms of an annoying yeast infection or a UTI, but yet it burned in a peculiar way. I made Brad aware of the issue. I carried on with our evening and stopped later at the store for some over-the-counter remedies.

We rang in the New Year of 2010 with enthusiasm and a great yearning to see what new things God would be doing. That year quickly turned into a critical time for me. It was apparently time for my lip service to stop; I needed to get out of my box and learn some difficult but worthwhile lessons.

A couple weeks passed and my "female pains" became worse. I knew it was time to see a doctor, so I made an appointment with my gynecologist. The first appointment was simple, and everything checked out great. I was given a prescription for a common drug to treat yeast infections. I had no visible symptoms the doctor could see but with the itching and pain, he suggested I was on the verge of "knocking out the problem." He instructed me to call with any further issues and on my way I went.

A couple weeks went by and the itching and burning pain became worse. There was something distinctive making me believe I was losing my mind. Every time I'd bend over, I'd feel an intense burning pain in one specific spot of the female area. Nothing made any sense to me. Everything about my symptoms was uncommon and random. I was back on the phone and again in the gynecologist's office for an exam and treatment. This time after seeing the nurse practitioner, I was given some creams to treat the symptoms of itching and burning and told I had contact dermatitis.

Those medicines didn't work either. Nothing and no one was helping me while the pain was only becoming more intense. After seven doctor visits, I had been wrongly diagnosed with a yeast infection, contact dermatitis, herpes, vulvodynia, and underwent a biopsy of the labia that came back normal.

My pain was horrible, embarrassing, and escalating by the week. It began to spread into my lower back, buttocks, and down my legs. I was having vaginal spasms, bladder spasms, leakage of urine, and odd vibrating and tingling sensations in my female area. Shooting pains were jolting in my bladder with other intimate symptoms occurring. I was unable to have sexual relations with my husband which made everything more upsetting for both of us. This experience was unbelievable. Somehow by the grace of God, I managed to go to work daily and complete my duties while suffering intense pain. I had no answers and I was running out of hope. In my deep despair and desperation I went to a new gynecologist to receive a third opinion.

I sat down on the couch in the doctor's private office after an exam, and sweat soaked my underarms. Worry overwhelmed me and fear ruled every fiber of my being. Dr. Chase had salt and pepper hair that was well groomed and matched his mustache. He wore a long white lab jacket with his name embroidered on the left chest. The desk he sat at was dark cherry and covered in papers. He held a pen in hand and wrote out prescriptions offering me medications for my pain and discomfort. I was direct with Dr. Chase and told him I needed answers and not just another medicine. When I asked him what was wrong with me, his words were this, "I don't see anything wrong or any reason for your pain. However, I've seen some of these symptoms in patients with multiple sclerosis, and I'm referring you to a neurologist."

I felt like I was hit by a Mac truck carrying concrete. I couldn't breathe and tears started to flow. My worst fear had become a reality. I immediately saw my life with no future. I had been concerned since I was eighteen when I suffered with optic neuritis that someday, I'd get MS and live bedridden. It was at the age of eighteen a neurologist told me I had a forty percent chance of developing MS later in life. Those words rolled around in my anxious and worried mind for years. Suddenly, I was reliving an emotional and painful past experience. I was now doomed. I had no known cause for my pain. I had a referral to a neurologist and a pending diagnosis of MS.

I called to schedule my next appointment, but the neurologist was over-booked and unable to see me for ten days. Since my situation wasn't considered an emergency, I had to wait. Ten days is unbearable to wait when you are in pain, have no answers, and feel like you are going to die. I became obsessed with the possible diagnosis of MS and researched everything I could to learn more. The more I read about MS, the more I became convinced I had it. I couldn't eat, sleep, or function normally. I became severely anxious, depressed, and an emotional train wreck, all while in tremendous physical pain.

Impatiently Waiting

In my heart of hearts I knew I had something wrong with me that was rare, and the doctors were missing it. I knew my symptoms could be caused by a variety of conditions such as; cancer, lymphoma, MS, spinal tumor, and more terrifying diseases. With persistence I searched diligently for answers on the internet. I wouldn't give up and my determination finally paid off. I put my one peculiar symptom into the Google search bar: "vaginal burning when bending over." This led me to some significant research on female disorders and eventually brought up a condition I had never heard of before called, "Pudendal Neuralgia." My heart raced and my respirations became fast and shallow while every word I read began to sound familiar. I had the exact symptoms. I printed out the information and handed it to my husband declaring a diagnosis.

Rock Bottom

We can't entirely understand all things we read or hear unless we experience them ourselves. It's impossible to totally relate sometimes. I empathize and sympathize with anyone who has a sleeping disorder. Due to a level of anxiety that could've bought me time in a mental facility, I was unable to sleep for over a week. When I lay down, my mind would race with excessive worry and negative thinking while my body would tremble in pain. My muscles would spasm in my back, and I had tingling in my hands and feet. At night I tossed and turned in bed until my physical body couldn't withstand one more movement. After hours of watching the clock, I'd immediately jerk up, shaking with a fast and pounding heart. I was experiencing severe anxiety and acute panic attacks. I was too familiar with the nature and effects of these anxiety attacks. Anxiety was something I had experienced on and off from a young age while being raised by strangers. During my childhood I was unable to explain or understand what was happening inside my mind and body, so I suffered silently with constant fear of dying, generalized anxiety, and panic disorder.

My first panic attack happened while we were eating at a restaurant called, Bonanza. Suddenly, I couldn't breathe or swallow. I almost choked on my food and felt dizzy, like I was floating away. I couldn't hide this attack, so I was taken to the emergency room. I was sent home after the doctor found nothing abnormal with my vital signs, EKG, or physical exam.

During this time of distress, I felt like I did when I was a child. I was at a loss for words, and no one was able to help me. I'd lie in bed at night and cry. I cried for help from my husband who supported me the best he could with concern and sympathy. But he had no answers. I cried out to God and knew He was there with me, but I wasn't feeling His presence. I talked to my friends and health care professionals, but they had no answers. Prayer was my greatest weapon, but I was emotionally exhausted and unable to do much of it for myself. Thankfully, I had family and friends who cared about me and encouraged me with their words and covered me in prayer.

The long awaited day arrived and my husband took me to my neurology appointment.

Dr. Adams was wise, experienced, and professional with a heart for his career and his patients. I knew I was in good hands. After Dr. Adams walked into the room, I choked back tears while I described what was happening to me and my paralyzing fear of MS. I was foggy headed and in a daze from not sleeping for a week, I was extremely emotional.

Dr. Adams performed a thorough and extensive exam. Some of it was simple testing and other parts were embarrassing and painful. He devoted time to evaluate me and listen closely to my complaints. When he was finished he sat down on a small stool next to us and explained what he found. All my neurologic testing came back normal and I had no signs or symptoms of MS he could see. I didn't present like the "usual" MS patient. He agreed that everything pointed to "Pudendal Neuralgia." He wrote me an order to have an MRI of my brain to rule out MS just as protocol. Dr. Adams also set up an appointment for me to visit a pain doctor to do a Pudendal nerve block to relieve some pain. I left his office with a glimpse of hope and a prescription for a sleeping aide. Slowly, I was finally getting somewhere, and I was extremely thankful as I looked forward to getting some sleep.

Careful Little Mouth What You Say

The pain doctor I saw next was unable to treat me with a Pudendal nerve block. She had no experience doing a block in the area where it needed injected. Dr. Luna examined me and suggested I be worked up for MS. With tears streaming down my face, I asked her if she thought I had MS. Her words were this: "I can't diagnose you because I'm not a neurologist, but from what I read in your chart and from my exam, it looks like MS." I was hopelessly confused.

When I got in my SUV I sobbed and cried hysterically. I didn't want to live the rest of my life with MS. As a nurse I had cared for bedridden MS patients before. My heart was shattered, my mind was spinning out of control and my body was weighed down with torment. With shaking hands I turned the key in the ignition and planned my way home in my head. I remembered the bridge I had to cross over. I was thinking that if I drove over the bridge and killed myself, I wouldn't have to live in anguish with a debilitating condition which would make me worthless to myself and my family. I started driving and when I got close to the bridge, I pictured driving over it. But I couldn't follow through with the action. I made it home safely by God's grace.

In pursuit of a diagnosis, I had multiple MRI's including one of my brain, lumbar spine, pelvis, and thoracic spine. All of these came back completely normal. The nerve pain medication the doctor gave me was only relieving a minimal amount of pain. I researched more on Pudendal Neuralgia and found a worthy article identifying specialists in the US and Europe who treated the condition. Impressed and thankful, I contacted a doctor's office in Baltimore, MD. The receptionist was helpful, concerned, and scheduled me an appointment for three weeks out.

A Ray of Hope

The day of my appointment couldn't have come fast enough. My wonderful and devoted husband took off work to drive and accompany me. The physician I met was the nicest, most compassionate, wise, and down to earth doctor I've ever met. He had an excellent bedside manner, and he genuinely cared about me and devoted himself to my care.

The whole day consisted of running tests in his office. The last test done was a temporary nerve block. While it was unbearable to have done with only local anesthesia, the relief I got afterwards made it worth the agony. He finally confirmed I had a diagnosis of Pudendal Neuralgia and not MS.

Dr. Mallone gave my husband and me a generous amount of information about PN. He explained the condition and how people can get it from a direct fall on their bottom, from long periods of sitting, bike riding, horseback riding, and even causes unknown. I may have also acquired Pudendal Neuralgia from the sexual and emotional abuse I endured while being raised by strangers. A lot of painful pelvic conditions can't be explained, but too many are linked to a history of sexual abuse. At that point the doctor made it clear the issue at hand was treating my pain and helping me to function normally again. I'd now have to learn a completely new way of living.

My first treatment consisted of three consecutive Pudendal nerve blocks done under CAT scan guidance at a specialty hospital. I had one every four to six weeks. The best expected outcome was for a decrease in inflammation and pain. Brad and I received a brand new perspective on my condition and on life.

Change of Life

The instructions from Dr. Mallone were explicit. I'd be living with a whole new set of rules and limits. Running is not allowed because it will aggravate the nerve and cause pain. I went from running four to six miles per day to only walking. Walking and swimming are the only safe exercises for PN sufferers along with some upper body strengthening. Ways to decrease pain and prevent major flare ups of the nerve are to take life easy and do nothing that hurts. Don't perform certain activities that will press on, stretch, or agitate the nerve: limited or no sitting, no heavy lifting, bending over, weight training, hiking, or excessive exercise.

Limited sitting is the hardest one for all of us who have PN. It is normal living to sit. We sit everywhere. We sit to drive, eat, some sit to work, we sit to watch TV, attend meetings and at church. We sit every day, and we sit often. The only time I now sit is to ride in the car, and I need to make sure my trips are short. Long distance driving will cause pressure on the nerve and can create pain and a flare up. I appear as an "outcast" in many places we go. When and where everyone else is sitting, I'm standing. We try to eat at restaurants that have bar stools with high tables so I can stand. At church I stand in the back of the room. We don't go to movies, and I miss out on other activities we enjoy because of this condition.

This disease is a chronic pain condition requiring a lifetime of avoiding stress, taking medications, possible physical therapy, and in extreme cases, surgery. Surgery is however the last resort due to its success rate and post operative healing time and pain. While there are treatments that may help relieve pain, there is no cure for PN.

Pudendal Neuralgia

Pudendal Neuralgia is a condition affecting the nervous system in and around the pelvic region. The symptoms of Pudendal Neuralgia are normally felt in the genitals, in the hips and thighs, and the buttocks.

It is not only difficult to have this condition, but it's shameful to discuss the problem because of its intimate nature. This disease affects one of the most sensitive areas of the body. The actual Latin word for Pudendal is the word "shame." The physical and emotional pain is enough to bear and knowing the Latin word makes me shake my head. We shouldn't be ashamed for a condition we have. We should be empowered to create awareness and have further studies done to help find a cure. We who suffer with Pudendal Neuralgia will not take this sitting down! (That is a little PN humor!) I continue to pray for healing from Pudendal Neuralgia. I don't know when complete healing will happen, but I have decided to trust God.

The PN website educates and brings awareness to a rare, debilitating, and embarrassing condition affecting both men and women. Please visit this site and take a moment to be enlightened about this disease, the symptoms, and its effects on people and their families: www. pudendalhope.org.

34

Therapy

$\mathcal{J}$t's a well known fact that stress plays a major role in our lives. It affects our thoughts, emotions, actions, and physical bodies. Stress can cause pain, increase pain, and make us sick. Dr. Mallone explained how living with constant stress and anxiety worsens pain. He advised I start therapy and get help with some lingering issues I needed to face. Some of my issues were deep-seated from being raised by strangers and from the abuse I endured. Dr. Mallone was right, so I began searching and praying for someone to help me.

This therapist was different from all the others. It was clearly evident I wasn't talking to someone who was just staring at me because it was their job to listen. Chloe was a true God-send. She was warm, understanding, and knowledgeable, a woman after God's own heart. Hand-picked by God to help treat me, she helped me more in my life than anyone else ever had. Each time I walked in her office I was able to see things from a different perspective, accepting things I couldn't before, and recognizing issues I was in denial about. During my time of therapy it became evident my eating disorder was more than a physical or emotional issue. It was also a spiritual condition the devil used to keep me in bondage.

My eating disorder was all lies from the beginning. Negativity and evil started working on my mind when I was a child. I believed the horrible things said about me and to me. The scale was an idol. I let the number define me as a person and hold me hostage. Thin girls, fitness magazines, models and nutrition became an obsession. Diets were my way of life. I never learned or knew how to eat normal portions or how to listen to my body. I listened to my emotions. If I was anxious, tired, bored, fearful, or hurt, food became my physical and emotional pacifier.

Chloe saw my brokenness and my deep desperation to be accepted and approved. I didn't have just health on my mind but the fear of becoming fat—an obsession to be thin. It's a deep seated mindset that's irrational but seen as logical by the person who believes it.

After a few sessions, I asked Chloe what her honest opinion was and what I should do. She told me straight out I needed in-patient treatment and hospitalization. I thought she was joking. Was she serious? I wasn't anorexic. I was eating, living my life, and functioning normally. Or at least I thought I was "normal." I looked at her with an intense and shocked expression asking, "Are you serious?" I expected her to say no. However, she told me I was on a downward spiral to a dangerous place, and I needed treatment. It was at that moment in time something powerful inside of me took over and gave me strength and hope. I felt righteously angry about my eating disorder. I wasn't willing or able to go to a hospital for treatment. In my heart I agreed with Chloe but I had a life to keep living, a job to work, and a family to take care of. How would I take off work, what would my family, friends, and everyone think of me? There was no way I was going to a hospital for treatment.

My eyes were opened for the first time, and I could clearly understand the situation. I was able to see how desperate, weak, and out of control I had become. I wanted to get better and truly break free from the obsessive thoughts, rituals, rules, and regulations. I was unwilling to continue with my life as usual. I told Chloe I couldn't go to the hospital, but I'd get better. I promised her I'd do what she said, and I was willing to do whatever it took. I specifically told her that God was going to do something in me, and He was going to work fast. The problem with eating disorders is this; most of us know we have a problem. But we don't know why or how to fix it.

My first assignment from Chloe was to pray over my scale and stop weighing myself. I also promised her I wouldn't binge and purge or "chew and spit" chocolate. It made me happy to know someone truly cared about me as a person, and I also appreciated and needed the accountability.

American Idol

The big white scale lit up with a bright red number every time I stood on it. It was my platform and the number was my audience who would applaud or "boo" me. I set the scale on my bedroom floor and prayed. I asked God to forgive me for making the scale an idol and putting it first in my life. I totally surrendered the scale to God and asked Him to heal me of my eating disorder. Streams of tears flowed and my prayers poured forcibly from my mouth. It was a powerful time of prayer and submission. I felt the presence of God and knew He was working in me and my heart.

To help me heal from my eating disorder, I read some extremely helpful books suggested to me by Chloe. My favorite one was called Life Without ED by Jenni Schaefer. This is an incredible story of how a woman relates to her eating disorder by giving it a name. She overcomes it by recognizing it, using psycho-therapy, and keeping a strong, courageous attitude to be an over-comer. I read other books helping me learn to eat normally and recognize my hunger and fullness signals.

Intuitive Eating by Evelyn Tribole is an excellent book, highly recommended by myself and the thousands of people it has helped. There are many resources available to us that will help more than we know. The truth is we have to want help. We have to recognize and admit we have a problem. We have to be ready and willing to surrender ourselves, our addictions and whatever else is holding us back in life.

Recovering from an eating disorder or any addiction is a long journey requiring patience and learning to live one day at a time. Mistakes happen; we all stumble and fall. It's important to get back up if we falter and move forward. It is not easy to give up something we based our lives on. It is challenging to reset our minds to the truth as we recognize the lies. I'm learning to change my position in life from kneeling over the toilet, to kneeling in prayer. – I need God a whole lot more than I need to binge and purge. This is where the journey of healing begins.

With the help of a sweet and wonderful dietician, I slowly learned truth about food and nutrition. My dietician Bonnie set up a meal plan for me and gave me freedom to eat chocolate. How could I not like anyone who told me it was acceptable to eat chocolate! Bonnie empowered me with knowledge about food and how other women just like me struggled with eating disorders. It's remarkable how we feel better when we know others are out there like us, and we don't suffer alone.

My eating habits were made up from things I read and believed to be truth. I ate foods because of what I read about them. I didn't enjoy or like them, but I ate them because they were going to help me be thin. You know those foods that help us burn calories and fat, those foods called "clean." The foods we eat when on a certain diet and the forbidden foods we can't eat. Bonnie taught me a new way of eating, how to eat what my body craved and what I liked. She reassured me it was normal to crave sugar, and encouraged me to go on an adventure of trying new foods. This was a new and exciting way of living for me. I was liberated to eat what I wanted and all my food rules and regulations went out the window. The "food police" were fired.

It was difficult to move outside my comfort zone but a little at a time I realized how I loved pizza and cheeseburgers. Don't misunderstand me, I couldn't eat whatever and whenever I wanted. Portion control is important and listening to my hunger and fullness cues. Those cues slowly came back to me. After ignoring them for years my body stopped telling me when I felt hungry or full. As strange as it sounds it's a common problem in the lives of people with eating disorders.

With God, time, and miraculous resources, I went eight months without weighing myself or binging and purging. I'm no longer in therapy, and I'm well along the path of recovery. I won't deny some setbacks. I've fallen a couple times but with God's strength I got back up. After a butt-kicking setback, I received an amazing revelation. God needed to reveal to me the motives and intentions of my own heart.

The last time I binged and purged, I was extremely out of control and fueled by negative emotions. Instead of praying and trusting God, I immediately ran to an old friend for help—food. After eating fifteen Oreo cookies, a half gallon of chocolate ice cream topped with whip cream and chocolate syrup, then twelve donut holes, I made myself vomit. Standing over the toilet I was shaking, feeling guilty, ashamed and out of control. I literally felt like I wanted to die. Something hit me in a profound way, and I saw what was happening to me physically, mentally and spiritually. Knowledge went from my head to my heart, and God gave me an epiphany.

What I learned was that every time I ran to food, it was an idol and something I trusted more than God. When I overate or binged and purged it created negative emotions and bad feelings inside me. Some of those were guilt, shame, worry, anxiety and uneasiness. Since I didn't want to live with those feelings I had to do something to make them go away. There were two options for me then: purging in the toilet or excessive exercising. After I purged I felt horrible; I was left emotionally exhausted. When I over-exercised for up to two hours on the treadmill I was physically exhausted. One wrong thought led to consecutive wrong thinking and actions. Food wasn't the answer to my problems, but it was my drug, my addiction - my quick fix. All of that hindered me in my walk and closeness with God. When I felt guilty it was difficult for me to want to spend time with a perfect, forgiving, and loving God. It is hard to accept grace when we don't feel like we deserve it. But that is just it, "For it is by grace you have been saved, through faith--and this is not from yourselves, it is the gift of God--not by works, so that no one can boast." (Ephesians 2:8-9 NIV)

When we invite Jesus to live in our hearts, our bodies become the temple of God. He makes His home in our hearts. Since God resides in us, we are to take care of our bodies so He can use us in mighty and wonderful ways.

"Do you not know that your body is a temple of the Holy Spirit, who is in you, whom you have received from God? You are not your own; you were bought at a price. Therefore honor God with your body." (1 Corinthians 6:19-20 NIV) It made perfect sense to me. I wasn't honoring God with my body. I was abusing my body and expecting to do great things for God. As soon as all this clicked in my heart I told God I was sorry. I told Him the absolute truth was I didn't want to live like that anymore. I want to be used by God to do great and awesome things beyond myself. I don't want to be held back by selfish acts of disobedience. I was and am willing and ready to give my all to God.

Now I have a true desire to eat and exercise in a healthy manner. I don't want anything to stand in the way of God being able to use me for greater purposes. I surrender all to Jesus.

Have I mastered all my eating disorder quirks and never battle the scale? NO! Have I ever again overindulged in ice cream, candy, cookies, or cake? YES! Do I look in the mirror every day and accept my body never comparing myself to any other woman? NO! I don't expect I will ever be 100 % free from all these things. But I am far better and much healthier than I've ever been.

We need to be realistic and acknowledge we live an imperfect life in a fallen world. What I know is this: God has brought me out of the darkness and into His glorious light. I can do all things through Christ who strengthens me; I am a new creation in Christ Jesus! I live my life for God and give Him all the glory. He offers and gives me everything I need; he died so I can live and have life in abundance. No chocolate or cake will ever do that for me.

Who am I?

After pouring my heart out to God, He spoke awesome words down into my spirit and He answered me. Let His words of love, hope, and security, comfort and strengthen you as it did me. "The sacrifice you desire is a broken spirit. You will not reject a broken and repentant heart, O God." (Psalm 51:17)

My prayer to God: Please accept my broken and repentant heart to you, Oh God. I am a sinner. I am yours. I offer myself to you for I am all I can give you. Just me! Do you want me, oh God?

Do you want to use me, God? Me? I was a poverty-stricken child, born into a mess of a world. I had a psychotic mother and a cruel and emotionally distant father. I was abused and torn apart by a woman called my "care giver." I lied, stole, manipulated, attempted murder, plotted evil, and sinned against my own mother! I obeyed the evil commands of people and committed disgraceful sins, stealing money, food, and property. I have fornicated, committed adultery, and abandoned my husband and children for a wolf in sheep's clothing. And in my despair, I ask you, "Who am I?"

Who am I that you would even love me? But you already died on the cross for me. Who am I that you would use me in this world to even glorify you or your kingdom? Who am I that people would see you in me? I am wicked and deceitful, a sinner.

God, they can't see me! They can't see the turmoil, trouble, anxiety, and stress. They can't see the pain, despair, heartache, and frustration. I am ashamed, I am scared, and I am embarrassed. Who am I that you would save a wretch like me? A Wretch!

Who am I?

This is God's response: "You are mine! You are saved by grace, washed by my blood, and cleansed by my righteousness. You are purified, justified, vindicated, created, and made for a greater plan and purpose than this world has for you. You were treated like garbage, a soul born into despair. Abandoned and left for the enemy to trample on, to mock, to torment, and walk on. The enemy saw you and knew you were a target. He had his eye on you and had plans to use you for himself. But I am God! I knew you before you were born. Created you and knit you together in your mother's womb. I spoke to you, appointed you, and chose you before you were born to do great works for me and my Kingdom! When the enemy realized my plan he was angry and tried even harder to destroy you."

"I snatched you up and out of the enemy's hand and began a good work in you. The enemy remains angry and comes to taunt you and tease. He reminds you of your past, your former days of old. But that is not who you are or ever who you were. Those are only things you have done and the sins you committed. You were always mine and always mine you will be!"

"I am sorry you are sad. I am sad with you. I am sorry you are frustrated. I am frustrated with you. But it's time once again to shake off these things that so easily entangle you. Seek first the kingdom of God and His righteousness and all else will be added to you! Cast your cares onto Me. Stop struggling and surrender all to Me. You are learning and growing. I care for you and love you more than you know."

What is in your heart? What does God say? God has promises for you. Don't let fear stop you from receiving them. Yes, He has great plans for you. So for now, trust and know God has a plan. God is in control.

"Trust in the Lord with all your heart and lean not on your own understanding; in all your ways acknowledge him, and he will make your paths straight." (Proverbs 3:5-6 NIV)

35
Loving God, Loving People

Being a nurse is rewarding and it gives me an opportunity to make a difference in people's lives. I don't go to work; I do a job for God. How is a day better spent than loving, caring, and helping someone? It is a privilege and an honor to have compassion and assist people on a daily basis.

I spent the first twelve years of my career working in hospitals, in acute care settings. I also worked for a physician in an office and currently for a same-day surgery center. While nursing is a rewarding career, it can also be stressful and exhausting. Bearing the responsibility of people's lives is challenging.

I've laughed and cried with many patients and families. I watched babies birthed into this world, and also held patients hands while they took their last breath. Patients have trusted me with their lives while I provided them with care. I've put bodies in bags and wheeled them into the morgue. I've medicated alcoholics and drug addicts so they wouldn't injure themselves. While the list is ongoing with what I've done as a nurse, there remain things I have not done. I have not lost my passion for what I do, nor have I lost my compassion for people.

When I started out as a new nurse in 1994 I worked at a hospital where nurses sat at the nurse's station on a midnight shift and giggled at an elderly woman. The woman was confused and continued to yell out silly things. With restraints on to hold her in bed and medication to keep her safe, she was alone in a dark room. My heart went out to this woman, and I went in her room to talk and provide some company. I was reprimanded by my co-workers who told me to leave her alone. They said I didn't understand yet but it was a waste of my time to be talking with her. Those nurses laughed at me and assured me that when I became a more "seasoned" nurse I'd understand. When I saw their lack of compassion for that woman it broke my heart. It was that evening I vowed to never become a nurse with those types of values.

At the second hospital where I worked, I had an exciting time gaining valuable experience and knowledge. I mainly cared for men as it was rare to have a woman patient there. We had a combination of medical patients which included those with acute strokes.

A man named Stephen was once a patient of mine who suffered a severe stroke. Stephen lay in the hospital bed with lots of tubing and wires. He was unable to talk, move, or do anything for himself. He was called a "total care patient." His food went through a feeding tube in his stomach. He wore a diaper for incontinence and needed to be turned from side to side every two hours to prevent bed sores. Stephen was only able to track people in the room and respond by blinking his eyes. Over time I began to talk to Stephen and pray with him. We prayed for his healing and also for Jesus to come into his heart. There appeared to be something in him fighting to get better, and God showed me that potential. I spent extra time with Stephen and was excited every time I saw the slightest improvement. Any improvement in him was miraculous.

Weeks went by, turning into months. Stephen made significant improvement and regained some important abilities. After intense therapy, he was able to talk with slurred speech, walk with a cane, and do most of his daily activities with minimal assistance.

Then that day came: the day we were anticipating with prayer and faith! He was released to go home. It was a joyous and inspirational moment; I personally wheeled Stephen out of the hospital and watched as he went home. Not only did he go home, but he was able to attend and dance at my wedding months later. This was a miracle and a blessing to witness. Take a moment to take in that true story of God's redemption, healing, promises, and love!

My job didn't go without struggles. I worked difficult shifts, and sometimes patients grew worse instead of better. Occasionally there wasn't enough help. The most difficult task, then and now, is working with negative and critical people. There is no avoiding them. They are everywhere. I once worked with Dorothy, a grumpy nurse. She shook her head at me often and told me many times I tried too hard and couldn't save the world. Dorothy would discourage me and make me feel bad. It is unfortunate I didn't possess the self confidence then to speak my mind.

However, I now have these words to say to Dorothy. "I may not be able to save the world but I can make a difference!" That is my heart's desire every day I go to work and in all I do. God, I want all I do to glorify you just as your word instructs; "Work willingly at whatever you do, as though you were working for the Lord rather than for people. Remember that the Lord will give you an inheritance as your reward, and that the Master you are serving is Christ." (Colossians 3:23-24)

36
Dead or Alive

y dad remained "buried," and I was living contently. But isn't it God's character to raise the dead back to life? God had a new plan. He opened the door for me to initiate contact and communication again with my dad. This made me feel awkward and vulnerable after finally feeling snug, peaceful, safe, and guarded.

I was having many vivid and revealing dreams about my dad from my childhood. Personally, God speaks to me through dreams and when that happens, I do listen. Apparently there was some unfinished business lingering around, and it was time for me to be obedient to God and do what he was telling me to do. I needed to totally forgive my dad and give him another chance to reconcile our father-daughter relationship. I sent the following message to my friends asking for prayer, knowing God would hear and answer us:

> Dear Friends,
>
> I've had some difficult struggles, trials and needless to say, ups and downs with my dad since childhood. I was released over one year ago to step back from him and sever our relationship to end his emotional abuse against me.
>
> I've prayed and prayed, and believe it is now in God's timing that I attempt to initiate contact to try to mend and rebuild our relationship. This is extremely hard for me considering everything I've been through. The

rejection, neglect, abuse, and pain he has caused me have been tremendous. I am willing – and I choose to – open my heart once again to my dad and humble myself knowing this will make me vulnerable and possibly set me up for more pain and rejection.

As a follower of Christ, I want to do God's will and walk in His best for me. With that being said, I will do whatever God is asking of me. I have to humble myself, but I can tell you pride rises up and wants to stand in the way. The guard I've put on my heart does not come down easily. So, I need prayer from all of you. I need prayer to be an over-comer, to be strengthened, to trust, and to know this is the perfect will of God. I need prayer for God to reveal truth to me and open my eyes to see with my spiritual eyes. I need prayer to accept whatever comes my way and to trust that all things will work out for good.

Please lift me and this decision up in prayer. Please pray for my dad who's unsaved and who condemns me for my Christianity. I believe, trust, expect, hope, and know that every word you pray, God will hear, answer, and honor. We are a people of God who He loves and adores! God bless you and thank you for your prayers. With the help of a trusted Christian mentor, I've chosen to write and send my dad a letter. We believe this is the best way to proceed with the first step.

Thank you! Love you all!!

Brooke

I sent out this prayer and then ventured to listen to God and prepared a letter to my father who would determine according to his choice whether we would have restoration or closure. Here is the letter I sent to my father:

Dear Dad,

I kindly ask you to please read, ponder, and accept this letter from my heart you hold in your hands. I've included some photos that Mom gave me. When I look at the precious photos of you and me together, I truly see in them a loving and caring dad who held me close to his heart and was happy having me.

I am taking the initiative to open up communication between us again. See, I've finally come to realize that I don't "need" you in my life. I can live without you. However, in my heart I've missed you, and I "want" you in my life. You are my dad and nothing can ever change that.

Last year when I told you I wasn't speaking to you again, I meant it. I was extremely angry and hurt. I needed to protect myself from you and the continuous hurtful, mean things you said. I let you manipulate and emotionally hurt me with your inconsiderate words and opinions. I had to take a stance for what I believed was right and guard my heart. At that time it meant having no contact with you. Time has given me an opportunity to think things over and to let my heart heal. This has been a time where I've been able to forgive you and realize you aren't perfect and neither am I.

I've been thinking a lot about our relationship, and there are some things I need to say. The first thing is why we have problems. We have never had a solid relationship built on anything trustworthy. Let's face the truth; you were not there when I was growing up. It doesn't matter who's to blame. The fact is that we were not together. When we were finally reunited, I was hurt and traumatized from living in an emotional state of pain, constant physical abuse, and some sexual abuse.

When I was given the opportunity to live with you, I had looked up to you more than anything in life. I thought my world would become perfect and you would be my hero. I put you on a pedestal even before I met you, and I convinced myself you would turn my life around. I failed myself when I set expectations for you that you couldn't meet. I expected you to approve of me, love me unconditionally, put me first in your life, accept me for who I was, and show me favor. Yes, you took care of me. You provided a way out for me from the tragic and disgusting life I was living in New Mexico. It was an amazing deed you did and as I've told you before, I do appreciate it. I know it put your marriage on the line with Janet. (Trust me, I heard the late night arguments you had about me coming to live with you.)

You provided for me physically with clothes, shelter, medical care, food, and other needs. But the critical things I needed and wanted so badly were lacking. My emotional needs weren't met. You spent more time hunting than you did with me. You spent more time yelling at me and calling me ugly names than you did encouraging me. You called me Ms. Moose, Fat Ass, made me run around the block, and said nasty things about Mom while you compared me to her all the time. All I wanted and needed from you was total acceptance and love. But with all that said, maybe I failed to realize and accept you did the best you knew how.

It has taken me a long time to say this and mean it, but I do forgive you. When I forgive you, I am also letting myself be free of all bitterness and anger which has controlled me and manipulated me for so long. I've been lost, hurt, and in pain from all the negative emotions in my life. I know you can understand and relate to me considering the pain in life you have also experienced.

All I want to say about Janet is this; she never wanted me in the first place. She resented me which clearly showed up in her words, tone, and actions. She also treated me differently from her sons. But I now can understand her fear and agitation. She was living with a man who she hadn't been married to long. And here enters Brooke, her teenage stepdaughter. This takes time, energy, and money from her while also stealing her attention. Maybe the wounds she caused weren't as deep or maybe since she was my stepmom it hurt differently, but regardless the hurt and pain she caused, it healed quicker.

You need to understand something. This junk between you and me has deep roots that developed a long time ago. Let me paint you a picture. You saw me last at the age of five and then not again until I was thirteen. I'm guessing you also had expectations of me. I wonder if you were hoping for and couldn't wait to see and take care of the "perfect daughter." A daughter who was beautiful, thin, smart, respectful, and all you dreamed of. I know I truly disappointed you in meeting any of those expectations. I came from years of abuse and dysfunction. I was torn apart and needed help to get my heart and mind right. I was rebellious, stubborn, and vowed to myself to never let anyone hurt me again. I'm sure I said and did things which were wrong, hurtful, and frustrating to you. For all of those things, I'm truly sorry. Some of those things were just me being a teenager, and some of those things were me being rebellious. Sometimes, I was living in a self preservation mode. I never knew who to trust, and honestly trust was never modeled to me.

The most difficult part for me is that you have never truly apologized for any of your wrongs. You have never admitted your faults. You rationalize your behaviors and wrong attitudes. You think I should accept you as you are, and it allows you to get away with being rude, obnoxious, and a jerk. This is unfair in a relationship with anyone. I don't understand how you can be so easy and lenient on yourself, but so hard and judgmental on me.

You have truly hurt me, Dad. And all I want from you is for you to care. I want you to understand, own up to your faults, and care.

You have said that calling me names and making me exercise was for my own good. But I became bulimic and still struggle with an eating disorder until this day because of what you said and did to me. Again, I take responsibility for my own actions, but you and Janet are part of the roots of it. Even some of my deepest insecurities stem from how you treated me. When I've tried to talk to you about any of this, you automatically get defensive and blame my mom. You yell and complain, insisting everything is her fault because she took me away from you and kidnapped me. Yes, my mom has faults. She caused me much pain. I totally understand this. But you both had problems and affairs going on that caused the huge mess. So, it took both of you to create the initial issues.

This is so frustrating. You just don't get it. We need to talk about the things of our past, own up to our mistakes, forgive so that a peaceful, non judgmental and non critical relationship can exist.

Regarding Mom, we have a relationship the best we can. I love my mom. It is that simple. I'm offering a relationship with you, too, and you are the one who gets to choose if it happens or not.

I don't know what your response will be. Will you roll your eyes at me for writing this letter? You may still refuse to listen to me and blame me for everything that has happened. Well, if you want to place all the blame on me, then you can have your way because there is nothing I can do if you believe that.

Life is short. I want to get to know you and have a true and meaningful relationship with you. I'd even suggest you and I spend a couple of days just the two of us so we can have some time to laugh and enjoy life together as father and daughter. I'm offering my hand and my heart to you as your daughter. You can choose to accept me as I am, or you can walk away. This time you get a choice. This time no one is there to take me away from you. You choose, Dad.

Love,

Brooke

Bridging the Gap

Three years have passed since I sent that letter to my dad. To my complete dismay I encountered the unexpected: his response to me was none. I have no doubt in my mind he received the letter with the photos inside. My words reached him and his heart. I know he chose again to deny and reject me. My son has contact with my dad and not long after I sent that letter, my dad mentioned the letter and told my son he won't have a relationship with me, because we can't get along. That was all he ever had to say about it.

That letter was a tool. It was a door of healing God opened to lead me through, a bridge I needed to cross over to get from fear to faith. I have now faced that fear, looked it in the eyes, and said, "I won't let you control me. I will no longer let you rule my heart or life." Fear and anxiety have been at the core of some of my words and actions for a long time. Time has been stolen from me. I hold up the shield of faith and stand upon God's word. I won't let this arrow penetrate my heart, soul, or mind any longer. I have the mind of Christ. I wear the helmet of salvation, and it guards my mind from the enemy. My father, Karl, will no longer direct my steps or actions in life; God will. This was a test of my obedience, a test of pride and a test of faith.

I have closure; I have peace. And I will continue to pray for that man to one day know Jesus and have a relationship with Him.

37
An Ordinary Girl

"*B*ut God chose the foolish things of the world to shame the wise; God chose the weak things of the world to shame the strong." (1 Corinthians 1:27 NIV)

I am no one, no one famous, that is. I am an ordinary girl living life with passion and a desire to do extraordinary things for God. I love life, family, friends, and people. I love to talk, give helpful advice, and encourage others. The beach is the most beautiful and amazing retreat in the world. Dogs are the cutest, loveable and greatest animal of all. No one's morning should ever lack a cup of light roast coffee with Splenda and cream. Exercise is wonderful and stress relief for my mind and body. My favorite hobby is getting a massage because it's the best relaxation ever. I hate to fly.

My pet peeves are drivers changing lanes without using their turning signal, and someone hanging up the phone without saying "bye." I am obsessively neat and organized and some would consider me a perfectionist. I've made many mistakes. I am by no means perfect, and I don't have the perfect family. My husband and I have our bad days and sometimes my kids drive me crazy. I think, do, and say things I shouldn't. I don't like to dress up, but would rather wear jeans and a T-shirt.

I've served as the children's praise and worship leader at our church. It is a true gift to watch children lift their pure hands and voices to God in worship. Children are free with their expressions and not much will hold them back. I love to help out with the children and youth whenever possible. The middle school and high school students have encouraged me tremendously with their strength, courage, and faith in God. I am excited in all the ways God uses me and allows me to be a part of his master plan. It is my passion to help the next generation become outstanding men and women of God.

My husband and two children are the greatest blessings in my life. I am honored to be a wife and mother. God has given me so much and being able to raise a family to serve and glorify Him is an extravagant blessing. As the only Christian home that currently exists on both sides of our families, I anticipate and expect God to do great things in and through us, and for generations to come.

It's not about me

Not one of us had a choice to be created, to be born, or to be given life. God is our Creator; He chose us. "You made all the delicate, inner parts of my body and knit me together in my mother's womb. Thank you for making me so wonderfully complex! Your workmanship is marvelous—how well I know it. You watched me as I was being formed in utter seclusion, as I was woven together in the dark of the womb. You saw me before I was born. Every day of my life was recorded in your book. Every moment was laid out before a single day had passed." (Psalm 139:13-16)

What we do with our life is important. Some choose to chase after the things of this world. Some gain pleasure from the lifestyle the world offers. Money, sex, position, fame, drugs, pornography, alcohol, and wild parties are common. The craving for them increases and intensifies, but they will never fulfill us. The Bible says, "And this world is fading away, along with everything that people crave. But anyone who does what pleases God will live forever." (1 John 2:17) I'm not sure about you, but I know who I am and what I'm living for: to make a positive difference in other people's lives. I want to please God and give Him honor.

I've seen and experienced God's salvation, restoration, healing, and magnificent power in my life. I don't know where I'd be today, or who I'd be, if not for God's hand upon me. All I can offer you is my honest and true testimony to help you see the awesomeness of God. If God has done these things for me, He can do them for you.

God sent his own son Jesus to die on the cross for my sins. He was mocked, beaten, and hanged on a cross to die a horrific death. Jesus rose from the dead three days later and is now seated at the right hand of God. I wasn't personally there to witness this, but I believe without any doubt this is true. If God would do such a wonderful thing for me, the least I can do is offer my life back to him. I do this by loving God and loving people. Why would I deny Him and refuse His gift of salvation? I've accepted and received eternal life with Jesus in heaven.

Every person has been born with a free will. It is by choice that we can believe, follow, and love God. The life we are living today is a result of the choices we have made in the past. When you take a look at yourself and your life right now, are you satisfied with where you are and what you are doing? Every new day is an opportunity to make right and better choices to improve your future. Today is a new day. What will you choose to do with it? The choice is yours.

No one is promised a perfect life of happiness, riches, great health, or a life without problems. We will all have struggles, battles to fight, and days when we won't want to carry on. The one thing that has given me hope, joy, encouragement, peace, and strength to overcome these trials has been Jesus.

Don't just take me at my word. I dare you to follow God with your own heart. I challenge you to ask God to prove Himself to you. God is faithful to His word and it says, "Ask and it will be given to you; seek and you will find; knock and the door will be opened to you. For everyone who asks receives; he who seeks finds; and to him who knocks, the door will be opened." (Matthew 7:7-9 NIV) When we seek Him honestly and diligently, we will find Him.

This is simply my life so far, touched and changed by God. I am looking forward with great expectation for the next new things God is going to do in and through me. The following is not only a prayer for me but also for you. I hope it becomes your desire:

> "I am compelled and energized by the power and strength of God to keep on keeping on. I want to move and walk into all that God has created me to become and do. It is not my will but His will I ask to be done. I surrender myself and pray for God to increase my faith, use the gifts and talents that He has put in me to pursue a life that

will touch and reach many in His name doing great things for His Kingdom!..... It's not about me."

Yes, hope has kept me alive, and His name is Jesus!

Eternity Matters

Take a look at the Ministry of Jesus. He preached, taught, delivered, cast out demons, healed people, performed miracles, and saved the world all by the age of thirty-three. Jesus had a three year active ministry over two-thousand years ago that still exists today! No words can describe the awesome power of the anointing from the Holy Spirit which was upon Him as the Son of God.

Jesus will reign forever and ever. Hearts and minds can't imagine or grasp the concept of eternity. On earth things die, they vanish, they cease to exist, and they end and become lost! In Heaven there is no such thing; there is only eternity. Eternity is a real forever place and a real forever measure of time we can't wrap our human minds around. But I tell you this, it is real and available for you and anyone who accepts and believes in the one and only Glorious Son of God, Jesus Christ. It is so beautiful, so awesome, and so profound!

Jesus wants you to "know Him." He wants a personal relationship with you. He wants to hold you close, love you, and be your best friend. He will change you, change your life, and freely give you the gift of eternal salvation. If you have never committed your life to him and asked him in your heart, it's a simple prayer of faith. Let's pray together:

Dear God,

I believe you sent your only son Jesus Christ to die on the cross for me. Jesus died in my place and gives forgiveness for my sins. I am a sinner, and I am sorry. Please forgive me of all my sins. I ask you right now to come into my heart and fill me with your love. Change me and my life. I want to live for you and with you for eternity. Thank you for this free gift of salvation. Thank you for your amazing grace, mercy, and love. Lead me in all my ways and grow me in my new walk with you.

Thank you, Jesus.

Amen.

About the Author

*B*rooke Lynn is a writer, nurse, and a health and wellness enthusiast. She transparently reveals her life experiences, struggles and triumphs with abuse, poverty, marital demise, parenting, and eating disorders helping others find the courage and strength for healing.

Brooke educates and creates awareness about eating disorders sharing her 26 year battle and recovery. She was an invited speaker for Cherished, a girls youth conference, and in December 2012 was the key note speaker for the IAEDP Foundation, promoting professionalism among practitioners treating those suffering from eating disorders.

Brooke has served as a children's praise and worship leader, worked with middle and high school students, and also served on church prayer teams with a heart for intercessory prayer. She passionately motivates others into a deeper level of faith while encouraging them to love and accept themselves. She resides in the Washington D.C. area, has been married for eighteen years and is raising two teenage children.

CPSIA information can be obtained
at www.ICGtesting.com
Printed in the USA
BVHW082229130919
558287BV00002B/88/P